Helion & Company Limited
Unit 8 Amherst Business Centre
Budbrooke Road
Warwick
CV34 5WE
England
Tel. 01926 499 619
Email: info@helion.co.uk
Website: www.helion.co.uk
Twitter: @helionbooks
https://helionbooks.wordpress.com/

Front cover: On Sunday 25 April 1965 four P-51D Mustangs conducted air strikes on the Presidential Palace and other rebel-held objects in the capital of the Dominican Republic. Two of the Mustangs are known to have been piloted by Colonels Rafael Reyes and Jorge Pichardo. (Artwork by Daniel Uhr, https://duhraviationart.com)

Designed and typeset by Mach 3 Solutions (www.mach3solutions.co.uk)
Cover design Paul Hewitt, Battlefield Design (www.battlefield-design.co.uk)

ISBN: 978-1-804518-70-0

British Library Cataloguing-in-Publication Data
A catalogue record for this book is available from the British Library

CONTENTS

Note: In order to simplify the use of this book, all names, locations and geographic designations are as provided in *The Times World Atlas*, or other traditionally accepted major sources of reference, as of the time of described events.

ABBREVIATIONS AND ACRONYMS

1J4	*Movimiento Revolucionario 14 de Junio* (14 June Revolutionary Movement)
AFB	Air Force Base
AMD	*Aviación Militar Dominicana* (Dominican Military Aviation)
ARD	*Armada de la República Dominicana* (Dominican Republic Navy)
CEFA	*Centro de Enseñanza de las Fuerzas Armadas* (Armed Forces Teaching Centre) (Dominican Army)
CIA	Central Intelligence Agency (US Government)
DEFCON	Defense Condition (US)
FAD	*Fuerza* Aérea *Dominicana* (Dominican Air Force)
GC	*Guardacostas* (Coast Guard)
IAPF	Inter-American Peace Force
ISZ	International Safety Zone (Santo Domingo)
JCS	Joint Chief of Staff (US)
LCI (L)	Landing Craft Infantry (Large)
LCU	Landing Craft Utility
LSM	Landing Ship Medium
LST	Landing Ship Tank
MATS	Military Air Transport Service (USAF)
NCO	Non-commissioned officer
OAS	Organization of American States
PRD	*Partido Revolucionario Dominicano* (Dominican Revolutionary Party)
PRSC	*Partido Reformista Social Dominicano* (Dominican Social Reformist Party)
PSYOPS	Psychological Operations (US Army)
PSYWAR	Psychological War (US Army)
SIM	*Servicio de Inteligencia Militar* (Military Intelligence Service) (Dominican Republic)
TAC	Tactical Air Command (USAF)
USAF	United States Air Force
USIA	United States Information Agency
USIS	United States Information Service
USMC	United States Marines Corps

ACKNOWLEDGEMENTS

The authors would like to express their deep appreciation to Albert Grandolini for having shared hundreds of pictures from his archives for this volume, the Dominican historian Luis Puesan for the invaluable data and also for the revision and correction of our text, to Mrs. Magdalena Cubas, daughter of Colonel Roberto Cubas Barboza, who was the commander of the Paraguayan Contingent of the IAPF in the Dominican Republic in 1965, for the precious data and photos for this volume. Mrs. Cubas also graciously shared her father's memoirs with the authors that contain unpublished data from this conflict.

INTRODUCTION

The name of the Dominican Republic has its origin in a Catholic Saint, Saint Domingo de Guzmán, who founded the Dominican Order, and the capital city is named after the aforementioned Saint. Dominican history is full of very peculiar characteristics, especially its long journey to independence. The Spanish took possession of the island from Columbus's first voyage in 1492, naming it *La Española* (Hispaniola). At the end of the seventeenth century, the French took possession of the western part of the island (now Haiti). The first attempt at Dominican independence occurred in 1821 but barely lasted three months, as Haitian General Boyer consolidated his domination over the entire island.

In the nineteenth century, Dominicans were not seeking complete independence like other countries; there were several attempts to annex the nation to other countries including the United States in 1865. Starting in 1838, a small group of Dominican revolutionaries began to conspire in order to achieve effective independence and free themselves from Haitian domination, but it was not until 27 February 1844 that independence was sought by Dominican patriots. The decades that followed were filled with tyranny, partisanship, economic hardship, rapid changes in government, and political exile. For several years the Haitians made several invasions (1844, 1845–49, 1849–55, and 1855–56) but were thwarted by Dominican forces. Incredibly, in 1861 a pact was signed with the Spanish Crown by which the Dominican nation once again became a Spanish colony, a unique case in the history of America. The purpose of this pact was to protect Dominicans from Haitian aggression. In any case, it did not take long for Dominican revolutionaries to begin fighting against the Spanish, who finally abandoned the island in 1865.

Independent life was not easy and there were numerous short governments led by regional leaders. The country was bankrupt due to accumulated debts and there was a threat of intervention from France and other European countries. Given this, at the beginning of the twentieth century, the US President Theodore Roosevelt carried out a military intervention in the Dominican Republic to avoid European intervention. In 1905, in an agreement signed between the American and Dominican governments, the Americans took charge of the Dominican customs and the tremendous debt that the country had.

During the first two decades of the twentieth century, the Dominican government did not guarantee the payment of debts with American banks, and the American companies that owned the sugar mills feared that the government did not guarantee their investments due to the constant threats of changes in governments. The Americans thus took possession of the customs by force when US President Thomas Woodrow Wilson (1913–1921) ordered the military occupation of the Dominican Republic. The United States

The Ozama Fortress in Santo Domingo during the first American military intervention (1916–1924) (left). United States Marine Corps troops in the Dominican Republic (right). (USMC Archives via Albert Grandolini)

Marine Corps landed on 16 May 1916 and took control of the country two months later. The military government established by the United States, headed by Rear Admiral Harry Shepard Knapp, was widely repudiated by Dominicans. The Dominicans refused to serve in the new administration. Censorship and limits were imposed on public speech but the occupation regime maintained most of the Dominican laws and institutions, reactivated the economy, reduced the Dominican debt, built a network of roads that finally interconnected all regions of the country, and created a professional National Guard. The most intense opposition to the occupation occurred in the eastern provinces of El Seibo and San Pedro de Macorís. From 1917 to 1921, American forces fought a gang of criminals in that area known as the *Gavilleros*. They dedicated themselves to looting and theft of livestock and they were joined by former Dominican soldiers but since they were not organised, they could not coordinate their attacks on the marines. They finally disappeared in 1921.

After the First World War, public opinion in the United States began to oppose the occupation. Then, President Warren G. Harding (1921–1923), Wilson's successor, worked to end the occupation, as he had promised to do during his campaign, and presidential elections were called in March 1924 in the Dominican Republic. The winner of these elections was former President Horacio Vásquez, who had cooperated with the United States to end the occupation. Vásquez's government was characterised by its corruption and misuse of government resources. In one month in power, they wasted 10 million dollars that the Americans had left in the state coffers. These actions led Trujillo to take power as the senior members of society became weary of Vásquez and his attempts to extend his period of government even further.

In 1930, the Commander of the Army, then Lieutenant Colonel Rafael Leónidas Trujillo, took advantage of the discontent that existed with President Vásquez to plot his rise to power, beginning a dictatorial period that would last with him in office until 1952

The US President Thomas Woodrow Wilson (1913–1921) (left). The American military governor in the Dominican Republic, Vice Admiral Harry Shepard Knapp (right). (Public Domain)

Dominican Constitutional President Horacio Vásquez (1924–1930) (left) (Public Domain). Before leaving the country, the marines formed a National Guard that was the base of the Dominican National Army (right). (Marine Corps University Press via Albert Grandolini)

The then Captain Rafael Leónidas Trujillo of the National Guard in 1922. Trujillo became the commander of the National Army and in 1930 he led a coup against President Vásquez. On the right, National Guard troops. (Albert Grandolini Archives)

but would continue with a series of puppet presidents until his assassination in 1961.

Between 1962 and 1965, political instability created the ideal climate for a new civil war, which would be the bloodiest in Dominican history, with a new American military intervention and also the Inter-American Peace Force (IAPF) sent by the Organization of American States (OAS), which is the central theme of this volume.

The volume is divided into four chapters: The first briefly describes the long government of Rafael Leónidas Trujillo and his successors until the outbreak of the civil war; The second chapter covers the organisation of the Dominican Armed Forces during the 1950s and 60s; The third chapter deals with the two antagonistic groups in the armed forces, the so-called Legalists and the Constitutionalists. Finally, the last chapter of Volume 1 describes Operation Power Pack conducted by US military forces. Volume 2 will cover the Inter-American Peace Force, the so-called 'April Revolution' day by day and finally the aftermath.

1

BACKGROUND

To understand the events that culminated in a civil war, also called *Revolución de Abril* (April Revolution) in 1965, Dominican political and military history must be put in perspective from the rise of Rafael Leónidas Trujillo and the presidents who succeeded him in power, until the outbreak of the Dominican Civil War.

Rafael Leónidas Trujillo

Rafael Leónidas Trujillo Molina was born in the city of San Cristóbal on 24 October 1891. Son of José Trujillo Valdez, a small merchant and Altagracia Julia Molina Chevalier, later known as *Mama Julia*. Trujillo was the third of 11 children. His siblings were Virgilio, Flérida Marina, Rosa María Julieta, José *Petán* Arismendy, Amable *Pipi* Romero, Luisa Nieves, Julio Aníbal, Pedro Vetilio, Ofelia Japonesa and Héctor *Negro* Bienvenido Trujillo Molina. Trujillo also had half-brothers on his father's side.

The only one of Trujillo's brothers who was in the military was his younger brother Héctor Bienvenido, whom Trujillo sent to study at a French military academy in 1935, when he was a Lieutenant. He then became a Generalissimo in 1959. The other brothers obtained the rank of General because Trujillo granted it to each of them.

Trujillo's childhood was relatively uneventful although his basic education was irregular and quite limited. In 1897, at the age of six, he was enrolled in the *Juan Hilario Meriño* school. A year later he moved to the *Pablo Barinas* School, where he remained for three or four years.

In 1907, at the age of 16, Trujillo obtained a job as a telegrapher, an activity he carried out for three years. Later, he dedicated himself with his brother *Petán* to rustling, forging checks and postal theft. For these crimes he was found guilty and imprisoned for a few months.

On 13 August 1913, at the age of 21, Trujillo married Aminta Ledesma Lachapelle, a young woman of good reputation, daughter of a farmer from San Cristóbal. They had two daughters: Julia Genoveva, who was born and died in 1914, and Flor de Oro Trujillo Ledesma, born in 1915.

In 1916, he again dedicated himself to criminal activities and led the band of robbers called *The 42*, feared for their violence. Then he stopped being a ruffian and worked for two years in the sugar industry as a country guard. That year, following the American intervention, the occupation army soon created a National Guard. In 1918, seeing an opportunity, Trujillo joined the newly founded military institution and was soon promoted to Second Lieutenant. On 11 January 1919, he was promoted again and took the oath, becoming lieutenant number 15 of the 16 that existed then in the National Guard. Trujillo received his training at the Haina Military School of the National Guard. On 22 December 1921 he was appointed to command the garrison in Seibo.

In 1922 he was transferred to Cibao and, while he was in San Francisco de Macorís, he was promoted to Captain without going through the rank of First Lieutenant, something irregular in the military ranks, but explainable due to the services provided by Trujillo to the American occupier. In 1922 Provisional President Vicini changed the name of the National Guard to National Police, and then in August 1927, it was called the National Brigade.

In 1923, before his appointment as inspector of the first military district, he participated as a student in the Officer School of the Northern Department. At this time, despite his military training, his political inclinations began to manifest. In his dizzying career in the military, he rose to the rank of major, and when US troops left the country in 1924, they left Trujillo in charge.

With the victory of Horacio Vásquez in the elections that followed the withdrawal of American troops in 1924, Trujillo remained at the head of the National Police. On 6 December of that same year, President Vásquez appointed him lieutenant colonel and chief of the General Staff. In the following year, he was promoted to colonel.

In 1927 Trujillo rose to the rank of general and became the commander of the National Brigade. On 30 March of that year, he married Bienvenida Ricardo Martínez, a young woman from Monte Cristi. A year later he met María de los Ángeles Martínez Alba, known as *La Españolita*, and had an extramarital affair with her. Rafael Leónidas, known as *Ramfis*, was born from this relationship on 5 June 1929.

The National Army was founded in 1928 by Trujillo during the government of Horacio Vászquez. In 1930, an insurrection against President Horacio Vásquez broke out in Santiago and the rebels marched towards Santo Domingo. Trujillo was ordered to subdue the rebellion, but when the mutineers reached the capital on 26 February, they met no resistance. President Vásquez learned that one of the ideologues of the insurrection was Trujillo himself and decided to resign as a negotiated solution to the crisis in order to avoid bloodshed. Vásquez was sent into exile and rebel leader Rafael Estrella was proclaimed interim president.

Rafael Leónidas Trujillo (1891–1961) at different stages of his life. (Public Domain)

Trujillo became the candidate in the 1930 presidential elections, taking Estrella Ureña as vice president. The opposition candidacy, represented by Federico Velásquez Hernández and Ángel Morales for the presidency and vice presidency respectively, withdrew, leaving Trujillo-Ureña as the only option.

The electoral campaign was carried out under a climate of terror caused by Trujillo and his paramilitary band called *The 42*, led by Army Major Miguel Ángel Paulin. Even the members of the Central Electoral Board were forced to resign on 7 May, being replaced by people who responded to Trujillo's will. The Trujillo-Ureña binomial won the elections on 16 May, officially with 45 percent of the votes. It was later learned that only 25 percent of voters went to the polls, which led to the belief that the elections were fraudulent. On 24 May 1930, Trujillo and Ureña were officially proclaimed president and vice president of the country, respectively. On 16 August at the age of 38, Trujillo assumed the presidency of the Republic.

On 3 September 1930, three weeks after Trujillo assumed power, the destructive Hurricane San Zenón hit Santo Domingo, leaving more than 3,000 dead. With money contributed by the American government, the city was rebuilt. In June of that same year, the opposition organised to overthrow Trujillo, but everything was in vain and the promoters ended up in exile.

In March 1931, General Desiderio Arias resigned from Trujillo's cabinet, who, being left without any opposition, strengthened his dictatorship. In October, Trujillo negotiated with the Americans to hand over customs in order to pay the government's debts and have access to money to rebuild Santo Domingo. He did not layoff or reduce salaries and instead readjusted the budget and public spending.

The Dominican Party was the ideological support machinery of the regime. Officially formed on 16 August 1931, it was the only party allowed during the regime, with few and temporary exceptions. Mario Fermín Cabral was the main sponsor of the party whose symbol was a palm. The party membership card became a mandatory document for all Dominicans of legal age and necessary for most daily activities, such as looking for a job or leaving the country. Given the risk of possible invasions by political exiles, Trujillo made a tour with his General Staff through the different provinces of the country accompanied by soldiers from the National Army on 31 December of that same year.

On 26 May 1933, he was named Generalissimo of the National Armies by the National Congress. In February 1934, a convention was held to elect Trujillo again as the Dominican Party's presidential candidate. On 16 May of that year and without any political opposition, the national elections were held with Trujillo as the only candidate. On 16 August, he assumed power for the second consecutive time, this time taking Jacinto Bienvenido Peynado as vice president.

Trujillo always showed concern about Haitian immigration to the Dominican Republic. In a large part of the Dominican provinces that boarded Haiti, the Haitians had more commercial influence. In October 1933 he travelled to Haiti to meet with its president at that time, Sténio Vincent. Trujillo proposed to Vincent to review the previous agreement of 1929 regarding the limits of the Dominican-Haitian border. Vincent accepted and in March 1936 both presidents signed a new agreement that established new borders.

He divorced Bienvenida Ricardo in 1935, claiming that she could not bear him children. However, in 1936, they had a daughter, Odette. Trujillo had two more children with María Martínez; Angelita Trujillo, born in Paris on 10 June 1939, and Rhadamés Leónidas Trujillo, born on 1 December 1942.[1]

One of the cornerstones of the Trujillo regime was the cult of his person. Since 1936 on, at the suggestion of Mario Fermín Cabral, Congress overwhelmingly approved changing the name of the capital Santo Domingo to Ciudad Trujillo (Trujillo City). The province of San Cristóbal was renamed Provincia Trujillo (Trujillo Province), and the highest peak in the country, La Pelona Grande peak, was renamed Pico Trujillo (Trujillo's Peak) in his honour.

Statues of "The Boss" were mass produced and erected throughout the country, and bridges and public buildings were also named in his honour. The country's newspapers wrote praise for Trujillo, as part of the cover, and the slogan 'Long live Trujillo!' was included on vehicle license plates. A neon sign with the motto 'God and Trujillo' was erected in the country's capital. Over time, even churches were ordered to advertise the slogan 'God in heaven, Trujillo on Earth'. As time passed, the order of the phrase was reversed to 'Trujillo on Earth, God in Heaven'. Trujillo was Catholic although his real devotion was superstitions.

In 1937, Trujillo met Lina Lovatón Pittaluga, a young woman from the upper class with whom he had an extramarital relationship and with whom he had two children: Yolanda, born in 1939, and Rafael, born in 1943.

From 28 September to 8 October 1937, a massacre of thousands of Haitians living on the Dominican border took place. It was known as the Parsley Massacre or *El Corte* and its *detonant* was economic rather than political reasons, in order to force Haitians not to use Dominican territory. At that time, even the Haitian currency had more circulation than the American dollar, which was the currency used by the Dominican Republic until 1947. It also has a lot to do with the social complexes that come from the Haitian invasion in the 1800s, and to pressure American mills to use Dominican labour instead of Haitian because it was cheaper. Dominican Army troops killed, according to estimates, between 15,000 and 20,000 people.

After the 1937 Haitian genocide, Trujillo began to have international problems, especially with the United States. Hamilton Fish, a member of the United States House of Representatives, asked his government to sever relations with the Dominican Republic if the conflict with Haiti was not resolved. On 31 January 1938, Trujillo signed an agreement with the Haitian government by which he committed to compensation of $750,000 for the massacre, of which he only paid $550,000.

During the Second World War, Trujillo sided with the Allies and declared war on Germany, Italy, and Japan on 11 December 1941. Although the Dominican Republic did not have direct military participation, this fact determined that the country became one of the founding members of the United Nations. In 1941, Élie Lescot, who had received financial support from Trujillo, succeeded Sténio Vincent as president of Haiti. Trujillo expected Lescot to be a puppet, but Lescot turned against him. Trujillo, unsuccessfully, attempted to assassinate him in 1944, and the Haitian government echoed the event in order to discredit the Dominican regime.

In February 1942 Trujillo was again nominated for the elections of that year by the Dominican Party and by the newly created Trujillista Party. On 16 May, the elections were held where almost 600,000 citizens voted, and Trujillo was elected president again. In 1944, on the 100th anniversary of the founding of the Dominican nation, Trujillo celebrated an event called The Centennial Celebrations.

At the end of 1945, discontent in the sugar mills worsened due to the inflation that existed at the time, aggravated by the salaries earned by low-skilled workers. Trujillo ordered the Army to carry out raids against those who dared to stay in their homes in protest, alleging the crime of vagrancy. Those captured were imprisoned and forced to work. These raids also included those who did not possess the regulatory documents required by the regime.

In January 1946, the Local Labour Federation, a group of labour protesters founded by union leader Mauricio Baez, went on strike that lasted more than a week. Although the dictatorship ended up giving in to the petitions of the plaintiffs, some of its leaders and participants were subsequently persecuted and murdered, while others were forced to take the path of exile. Sometime later Trujillo disintegrated all the unions in the country, forcing them to belong to a federation related to him.

On 4 August 1946, a strong earthquake hit the northeastern region of the country. This earthquake produced a 16-foot (five-metre) high tsunami on the coast of Scottish Bay that caused the death of almost 2,000 people.

In May 1947, new elections were held, this time tinged with strong international criticism of the dictatorial nature of the government, which forced Trujillo to mount a democratic fiction. Three political parties participated in these elections, the National Labour Party, the Democratic National Party and the Dominican Party, whose candidates were Rafael A. Espaillat, Francisco Prats Ramirez and Rafael Trujillo, respectively. Trujillo ended up winning the contest with 90 percent of the votes.

Trujillo had to face two guerrilla movements that wanted to overthrow him. The Dominican exiles held a congress at the University of Havana and formed the so-called 'United Front of Dominican Liberation' with Ángel Morales as president. Its main motive was to arrange military aid to the democratic governments of Latin America and the Caribbean to use it against the Trujillo dictatorship. Among the members was the Dominican storyteller and politician Juan Bosch, who took on international efforts and travelled to several countries to meet with their respective presidents. On 21 September 1947, the group of Dominicans in exile, along with a volunteer battalion of armed soldiers from Cuba and other Latin American countries, left for Santo Domingo in a military movement called the Cayo Confites Expedition. The expedition failed; The expedition members were forced to disembark, and then be arrested and taken to the Columbia military compound, located in Havana. Two years later, in 1949, the Luperón Expedition arose, whose base was established in Guatemala. On 19 June of that year the Dominican revolutionaries left with six transport aircraft and a good number of weapons, but bad weather caused four aircraft to land in Cozumel, Mexico and one more returned to Guatemala, so only one aircraft with just 15 guerrillas arrived in the Dominican Republic. In a very short time, the Dominican Army killed 10 of them, capturing the other five. They were sent to prison after a trial but released after nine months and expelled from the country.

In 1950 Mauricio Baez was kidnapped in Cuba where he was exiled and his whereabouts were never known again. In October 1952, Trujillo created the Trujillonian Institute with Manuel A. Peña Battle as its president. The institution's mission was to disseminate the work of Trujillo's government.

At the end of the 1950s, during the Trujillo regime, a type of secret police called the Military Intelligence Service (*Servicio de Inteligencia Militar,* SIM) was created whose purpose was political repression. The organisation had several secret agents and officials of the dictatorship with Johnny Abbes as its leader. In many cases, Abbes was in charge of carrying out Trujillo's orders of repression and torture, although many claim that sometimes Abbes acted on his own. The SIM frightened the general population through torture and had several places to carry out such acts, including the 9th Prison and the 40th Prison.

Trujillo encouraged diplomatic and economic relations with the US, but maintained tense relations with parts of Latin America, especially Costa Rica and Venezuela. He maintained friendly relations with Franco in Spain. At the international level, the regime prioritised, through the secret police, attacks against preeminent opposition figures abroad, among them the attack on Venezuelan President Rómulo Betancourt in 1960, and the kidnapping of the Spaniard Jesús Galíndez Suárez, in the United States, on 12 March 1956. He also maintained strong ties with the Somoza dictatorship that reigned in Nicaragua and Batista in Cuba.

Towards the end of his administration, his relationship with the United States deteriorated again. On 12 March 1956, by orders of the dictatorship, the Spanish exile Jesús de Galíndez, a professor at Columbia University and who at that time lived in New York, representative of the Basque government in exile, was kidnapped. Galíndez had written a doctoral thesis on the dictatorship of Rafael Leónidas Trujillo and, when he found out, he had him kidnapped, later making him disappear. This fact caused the United States to definitively break relations with the dictatorship.

Trujillo was a dynamic and healthy person although as he grew older, he had prostate problems and frequent urinary infections. Trujillo acquired numerous properties and carried out very lucrative businesses. He and his family amassed enormous wealth. He acquired properties including large-scale cattle lands and became involved in meat and milk production, operations that soon evolved into a monopoly. Other industries owned by him included sugar, salt, tobacco, wood and lottery. By 1937, Trujillo's annual income was around a million and a half dollars and by 1940 he had already taken over most of the Dominican companies, creating a monopoly in the country. By 1960 he owned 60 percent of the Dominican sugar industry.

Trujillo reorganised the State and the economy while carrying out extensive construction work on large infrastructure projects in the Dominican Republic. His dictatorship ended with the political instability resulting from *caudillismo* carried over from the nineteenth century, which was reflected in a certain prosperity and modernity for the Dominicans, although much of the wealth generated in the country during that period ended up in the hands of the dictator and his relatives. This relative economic development was accompanied by the restriction of civil rights and liberties that were practically non-existent throughout his regime.

He was popularly known as *El Jefe* (The Boss) or *El Benefactor* (The Benefactor), but also by less flattering nicknames such as *Chapita* (metal sheet), due to his fascination with medals. Dominican children emulated him by building toy medals out of bottle caps. He was also known as *El Chivo* (The Goat).

On 22 December 1958, between Jimaní and Malpasse, on the Dominican-Haitian border, Trujillo and François Duvalier signed a mutual protection agreement. The agreement established, among other things, that neither of the two governments would allow subversive activities against any of them in their respective territories, nor those political exiles would carry out systematic propaganda inciting the use of violence against their respective states. That same year, when Trujillo realised that Fidel Castro was gaining ground, he began to support the dictatorial regime of Fulgencio Batista by providing it with armament and ammunition. Trujillo, convinced that Batista would defeat Castro, was very surprised when he presented himself as a fugitive, after being overthrown. Trujillo kept Batista as a virtual prisoner until August 1959, and after paying one million dollars for the armament and ammunition sent to Cuba before, Batista was finally able to travel to Portugal, a country that had granted him a visa.

The dictator was used by the US government to try to overthrow the then nascent revolutionary government of Fidel Castro. For his part, Fidel Castro threatened to overthrow Trujillo, and he responded by increasing the budget for national defence. A foreign legion was organised to defend Haiti, given the possibility that Castro would first invade the western part of the island to overthrow the regime of François Duvalier.

On 14 June 1959, several armed men commanded by Enrique Jiménez Moya landed in Constanza with the aim of overthrowing Trujillo. Days later, on 20 June, some 144 men led by José Horacio Rodríguez landed in Maimón in the province of Puerto Plata, who arrived on a boat called *Carmen Elsa*. After several days of combat against the regime, the expedition members were defeated and transferred to San Isidro Air Base, where they were tortured. Some survived, but most were later shot.

That same year, a left-wing political group called *Movimiento 14 de Junio* (14 June Movement/1J4) was formed in the country, made up of young people who sought a change towards the democratisation of the country. The movement had Manolo Tavárez Justo and his wife Minerva Mirabal as leaders. The Trujillo regime was cruel towards most of the group's members and the SIM was responsible for persecuting, imprisoning and torturing them.

When John F. Kennedy took office as president of the United States on 20 January 1961, the plans of the Central Intelligence Agency (CIA) to overthrow Trujillo were already underway. Despite this, President Kennedy sent diplomat Robert D. Murphy to meet

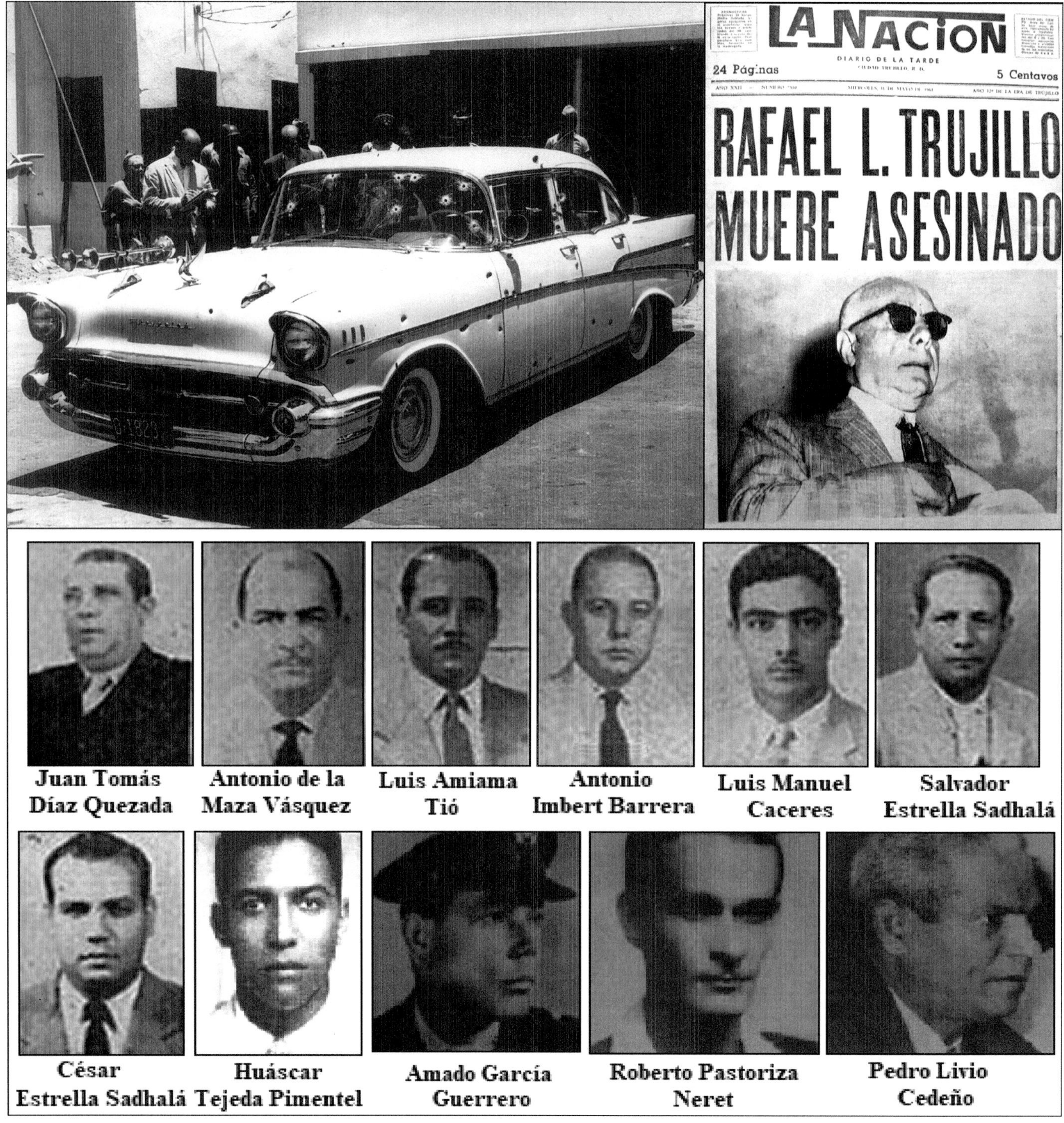

Trujillo's bullet-riddled 1957 Chevrolet Bel Air sedan (top left). (Albert Grandolini Archives). The cover of the Dominican Republic newspaper *La Nación* announcing the assassination of Trujillo (top right). The murderers of the former president (bottom). (Public Domain)

with Trujillo and persuade him to step down from power. Murphy arrived in Santo Domingo on 15 April 1961, being the fourth and last emissary of the US government who tried to convince Trujillo to withdraw from power, an approach that was ignored by the dictator.

For the 30 May plot, the United States government offered its support in weapons and logistics to those seeking to end the dictatorship, but did not maintain its support after the assassination of the tyrant. Although the plan ended Trujillo's life, it also meant the death of almost everyone involved, as they were isolated without international support.

The dictator had become an embarrassment to the United States, a situation that became increasingly tense following the attack against Rómulo Betancourt. On Friday, 25 November 1960, the brutal murder of the three Mirabal Sisters, Patria, Minerva and María Teresa, opponents of the dictatorship, further increased discontent towards it.

On Tuesday, 30 May 1961, at 9:45 pm, at kilometre nine of the highway from Santo Domingo to San Cristóbal, the car in which Trujillo was travelling was machine-gunned in an ambush plotted by Modesto Díaz, Salvador Estrella Sadhalá, Antonio de la Maza, Amado García Guerrero, Manuel *Tunti* Cáceres Michel, Juan Tomás Díaz, Roberto Pastoriza, Luís Amiama Tió, Antonio Imbert Barrera, Pedro Livio Cedeño and Huáscar Tejeda. The vehicle, a Chevrolet Belair 1957, received more than 60 bullet impacts of various calibres, of which seven hit the dictator's body, causing his death. His driver, Zacarías de la Cruz, received several hits, but did not lose his life, although he was left for dead by the executioners.

The weapons provided by the CIA had been hidden by Lorenzo Berry (known as *Wimpy*) and the American Simon Thomas Stocker, owner of the only supermarket in the country and resident in the Dominican Republic since 1942. Both men were CIA contacts in the country. Stocker refused CIA remuneration for his efforts, citing his moral convictions. The weapons were hidden for more than two months, at personal risk and that of his family, inside a small closet in his studio, in his private residence, which was located on a lot on the south side of Independencia Avenue next to Máximo Gómez Avenue. The weapons were indeed used to kill Trujillo.

Hours after Trujillo's death, his son Ramfis, who was in Paris, rented a plane and returned to Santo Domingo in the early hours of Wednesday, 31 May, immediately putting himself in charge of the situation and becoming the strong man of the country, despite the fact that Joaquín Balaguer still formally headed the presidency.

The SIM and the other state security services carried out extensive raids in all sectors of the city, searching for the perpetrators. On 2 June 1961, SIM agents broke into the house of Lieutenant Amado García Guerrero, who was murdered by several machine gun shots. On 4 June of that same year, two other suspects were murdered, Juan Tomás Díaz and Antonio de la Maza. On 10 June General José René Román Fernández *'Pupo'*, who served as Secretary of the Armed Forces of the dictatorship, was arrested and tortured, when his connection to the plot was known. On 18 November, Roberto Rafael Pastoriza Neret, Pedro Livio Cedeño Herrera, Luis Salvador Estrella Sadhalá, Modesto Díaz Quezada, Huáscar Antonio Tejeda Pimentel and Luis Manuel *'Tunti'* Cáceres Michel who had been captured days after Trujillo's assassination, were all taken to the Hacienda María in San Cristóbal and were shot by Ramfis Trujillo.

Trujillo's funeral, held on 2 June, was that of a true statesman and a long procession accompanied him from the National Palace to the town of San Cristóbal, where he was buried. Thousands of people from all social strata paraded before the coffin with Trujillo's remains. The then President Joaquín Balaguer gave the laudatory speech, saying, among other things:

> The moment is therefore propitious for us to swear on these beloved relics that we will defend their memory and that we will be faithful to their slogans while maintaining unity. Dear boss, see you later. Your spiritual children, veterans of the campaigns you waged for more than 30 years, we will look towards your tomb as a standing symbol and we will not omit any means to prevent the flame that you lit on the altars of the Republic and in the souls of all from being extinguished. the Dominicans...[2]

President Joaquín Balaguer in 1960, with a portrait of Rafael Leónidas Trujillo behind (left). General Ramfis Trujillo (right). (Public Domain)

The Trujillo family stayed in the country until August of that year, and they were able to leave the country freely via Pan American planes. Ramfis Trujillo had to remove his father's body. Trujillo was buried in Paris, in the Père-Lachaise Cemetery, at the request of his family.

On 19 November, the military uprising known as The Pilots' Rebellion took place. This, together with international pressure, prevented Trujillo's brothers, *Negro* and *Petán*, from taking over the government aided by Army officers. Ramfis had already left the country. General Pedro Rodríguez Echavarría, head of the Northern Command of the Dominican Air Force joined President Balaguer to try to unify the government into a civic-military junta but this attempt succumbed in 24 hours to efforts by officers who later formed the Constitutionalist movement. Echavarría and his brother who was the head of the Air Force were sent into exile, and Balaguer went into self-exile. A provisional government was formed and called elections for 20 December 1962.

These elections were the first with characteristics of democratic plurality and where political parties came to play a significant role. The elections gave victory to Juan Bosch, presidential candidate for the Dominican Revolutionary Party (*Partido Revolucionario Dominicano*, PRD) with 59.5 percent of the votes.

Héctor Bienvenido Trujillo Molina

Héctor Bienvenido Trujillo Molina, Rafael Leónidas Trujillo's brother, was known as *El Negro* (The Black One). He was president of the Dominican Republic twice, the first as interim president from 1 March to 1 October 1951 and as President of the Republic from 16 August 1952 to 3 August 1960. He was born in San Cristóbal in 1908 and died in 2002 at the age of 94 in Miami. During his brother's long presidency, he served as Secretary of War, Navy and Aviation.

When Rafael Trujillo left power in 1952, Héctor was elected president but the strings of power continued to be pulled by his older brother, so Héctor was considered a puppet president. In the elections of 1957, Héctor was re-elected but in 1960, trying to soften the sanctions of the OAS, and the United States, Rafael Trujillo made his brother *Negro* resign and the jurist Joaquín Balaguer remained as puppet president.

President Héctor Bienvenido Trujillo Molina (1952–1960). (Public Domain)

Joaquín Antonio Balaguer Ricardo

Joaquín Antonio Balaguer Ricardo was born on 1 September 1906 in Villa Bisonó, Santiago and passed away in Santo Domingo on 14 July 2002 at the age of 96. He was an essayist, writer, statesman, poet, politician and Dominican president in the periods 1960–1962, 1966–1978 and 1986–1996, making him the politician who held the position the most times in the Dominican Republic.

Throughout three decades of work as a pro-Trujillo politician, Balaguer was alternately seen as both an employee of the regime and a distinguished collaborator close to Trujillo. When Trujillo arranged for his brother Héctor Bienvenido to be re-elected to the presidency in 1957, he chose Balaguer as vice president. Three years later, Trujillo forced his brother to resign to improve the image of his regime internationally and show that the Dominican Republic could have a president not related to the Trujillos, and Balaguer succeeded him. However, Balaguer had practically no power and was considered a mere puppet of Trujillo.

When Trujillo was assassinated in 1961, and despite having long been a collaborator of the dictator, Balaguer took measures to free the country from the regime by granting some civil liberties and relaxing the strict censorship to which Trujillo had the press subjected. The OAS was satisfied and lifted the economic sanctions imposed on the Dominican Republic. Balaguer was only able to retain power until 16 January 1962.

During the period 1962–1964 the Dominican Republic only had seven months of full democracy, under the presidency of Juan Bosch.

President Joaquín Antonio Balaguer Ricardo in his first presidency (1960–1962). (Public Domain)

When a military coup overthrew Bosch, the country began a tumultuous period that led to the civil war of 24 April 1965, topic that is covered in the corresponding chapter in this volume. In 1966, Balaguer took over the presidency again and had to lift a country devastated by the civil war.

A Collection of Presidents

In a short period between 1962 and 1965, the Dominican Republic had no fewer than nine presidents, namely:

- Huberto Carlos Bogaert Román, who just stayed in the post for two days, 16–18 January 1962.
- Rafael Filiberto Bonnelly Fondeurl, who remained in power from 18 January 1962 to 27 February 1963. He organised the first truly democratic elections in the Dominican Republic.
- Juan Emilio Bosch Gaviño, elected president in the first democratic elections in the country but stayed in office for only seven months (27 February to 25 September 1963). Bosch immediately carried out a profound restructuring of the country. On 6 April, a new liberal constitution was promulgated that granted rights unknown to Dominicans. Bosch faced traditionally powerful sectors. His attitude against the large estates brought him the animosity of the landowner sector. The Catholic Church believed that Bosch was trying to secularise the country. The industrialists were suspicious of the benefits that the new Constitution granted to the working class. The military, who previously enjoyed the freedom to do whatever they wanted, felt that Bosch was subjugating them. Bosch was overthrown by a coup led by the head of the armed forces General Víctor Viñas Román and Colonel Elías Wessin y Wessin and replaced by a three-man military junta.
- Major General Víctor Elby Viñas Román, President of the Provisional Government Board formed by the senior officers of the armed forces, who just stayed in power for one day, 25–26 September 1963.
- Emilio de los Santos Salcié, President of the triumvirate that led the country after the overthrow of President Bosch. The triumvirate cabinet was made up of right-wing politicians and individuals linked to the business community. In December 1963, a guerrilla group led by Manuel Aurelio Tavárez Justo and the leaders of the 14 June Political Group (1J4) revolted in the mountains to fight against the triumvirate. The guerrillas were quickly surrounded by Army troops and forced to surrender. Once taken prisoner, almost all of them were murdered and only a few were spared. When President Emilio de los Santos found out what had happened, he immediately resigned from his position declaring that he would not be an accomplice in the murder of a group of young people, having given instructions to preserve their lives.
- Manuel Enrique Tavares Espaillat and Ramón Tapia Espinal were the other two members of the triumvirate who took over the Presidency between 22 and 28 December 1963.
- Donald Joseph Reid Cabral was chosen to lead the government when Santos resigned. He had not been involved in the Bosh coup, and he did allow corruption in the ministers and the military. He was not a puppet president and he enjoyed military support.
- Dr. Rafael Molina Ureña, designated by the Constitutionalist Military Command as Provisional President of the Republic on 25 April 1965. Moments later, the reestablishment of the 1963 Constitution and the return of Professor Bosch that same day from Puerto Rico was announced, and that ignited the civil war. Molina Ureña just stayed two days on the presidency. During that conflict, the country had two parallel governments, a military junta led by the Air Force Colonel Pedro Bartolomé Benoit Vandehorst and the so-called "constitutional" government led by rebel Colonel Francisco Alberto Caamaño Deñó.

Between 28 April and 1 May 1965, there was a power vacuum in the initial days of the civil war.

Presidents between 1962 and 1965, the result of the deep political crisis in the Dominican Republic. (Public Domain)

2

THE DOMINICAN ARMED FORCES IN THE 1950s AND 1960s

Dominican National Army (*Ejército Nacional Dominicano*, END)

As a more distant precedent, the so-called Republican Guard had been created in the 1860s. In 1905, a Rural Guard was created with a military structure but with police functions. There was no military academy until the Americans created one in 1920. The Dominican officers before were members of rich families, many without military training, for that reason the Americans were able to defeat them easily in 1916.

On 14 May 1917, the Dominican National Guard (GND) was created, which in 1921 became the Dominican National Police (*Policía Nacional Dominicana*, PND). By 1927, the PND was renamed the National Brigade (BN) and finally through Law No. 928, of 17 May 1928, the National Brigade was renamed National Army (EN).

In the mid-1930s under the government of Rafael Leónidas Trujillo the National Army was completely reorganised and its structure would remain basically the same for decades. The armament available to the Dominican Army in 1935 consisted of: a Citroën-Schneider CA1 tank, the first tank of the Dominican Army, assigned to the Artillery and Machine Gun Company of the *Generalissimo Trujillo* Regiment; Colt 7mm, Browning .30 cal, Vickers .30 cal; Thompson .45 cal, and similar machine guns and submachine guns; 37mm Hotchkiss cannons, 10mm Salva, 75mm Krupp, as well as mortars and other small-calibre cannons. The Army during this time also used a wide variety of rifles and pistols, including the Remington, Browning Automatic Rifle, Springfield Model 1903, Mauser Model 1893 and even Krag-Jørgensen rifles.

The total number of effectives of the Army in 1937 was 3,839 troops, including the police. In 1942 the Army had 3,500 men and the police 900, armed with 2,409 Mauser Model 1893, 1,800 Krag-Jørgensen M1898, left by the US in 1924, 38 Springfield guns, 13 mortars, 27 Browning machine guns, 49 Thompson machine guns, 1,765 pistols and revolvers.

By 1937, the National Army was made up of a General Staff, Auxiliary Corps, Intelligence Service, the President Trujillo Teaching Centre, Radiotelegraphy and Signals Detachment, Aviation Detachment, Quartermaster Detachment, Navy, Corps of Engineers, Music Band, Artillery and Machine Gun Company, Cavalry Squadron and 27 infantry companies. The forces stationed in Santo Domingo were grouped in the *Generalissimo Trujillo* Regiment, formed by the staff described above, the *Ramfis* Regiment commanded by the Quartermaster General and formed by the Radiotelegraphy and Signals Detachment, the Navy Detachment and the 17th Company, while the Headquarters Detachment, Music Band and the Departmental Arms Intendance were under the control of the Headquarters Adjutant.

Table 1: Forces of the National Army in 1937

Supreme Chief Generalissimo (Rafael L. Trujillo)	A Major General, as Secretary of the Interior, Police, War and Navy and a Brigadier General, Assistant to the Secretary.
General Staff of the National Army	A Chief of Staff Brigadier General, an assistant of the General Staff Colonel, three Lieutenant Colonels, a Law and Intelligence Officer Major, four Majors and six Captains as assistants of the General Headquarters, two Staff Major Sergeants, 10 Major Sergeants, a Staff Sergeant, a Second Sergeant, two Second Corporals of the General Staff, and three Privates.
General Quartermaster	A General Quartermaster Lieutenant Colonel, an assistant Captain, three First Lieutenants, as Quartermasters of the North, South and Weapons Departments, four Second Lieutenant Accountants, a First Sergeant, a Quartermaster Sergeant Major, an accountant Sergeant Major, two Accounting Assistants Major Sergeants, four Section Manager Sergeants, eight Second Corporals, a Cook; a Private as Barber, a Machine Technician Private, eight privates and 25 conscripts.
Medical Corps	A Medical Corps Director Lieutenant, two Medical Inspector Captains, an Assistant Director Captain, three Assistants of the Medical Corps First Lieutenants, 13 Medical First Lieutenants, three First Lieutenants dentists, four Second Lieutenants Doctors, two Second Lieutenants Pharmacists, three Medical Corps Sergeants, 28 Medical Corps Corporals and 40 Privates.
Corps of Engineers	A Major as Commanding Officer, a Captain as Adjutant, an inspector First Lieutenant, two Draftsmen Major Sergeants, an Accountant Major Sergeant, two First Sergeants, a Second Sergeant, an Electrician Sergeant, a Storekeeper First Corporal, an Inspector First Corporal, two Inspector Second Corporals, 15 Second Artisans, 16 Third Craftsmen and 25 conscripts.
Music Band	A Director Captain, a Deputy Director First Lieutenant, a Principal Musician, eight Musicians 1st class, 12 Musicians 2nd class, 18 Musicians 3rd class, 15 Musicians 4th class and a Drum Major.
Transportation Detachment	A Captain Commander, a Workshop Manager First Lieutenant, a Second Lieutenant, a Chief Mechanic Second Lieutenant, a First Sergeant, a Sergeant, five Driver First Sergeants, four Sergeants First Class Mechanics, a Sergeant Second Class driver, three Truck Driver Sergeants, a First Corporal driver, five Mechanical Corporals, four Truck Drivers, a Corporal First Electric Welder, a Corporal First Carpenter, two Second Mechanical Corporals, four Corporals, 32 bus driver conscripts, 15 Private Mechanics Assistants, 45 Automobile drivers, a Saddler, a tinsmith, a Cook, a Cornet, 20 Motorist conscripts, a barber conscript and 12 conscripts.
Radiotelegraphy Detachment	A First Lieutenant, a Technical Sergeant, three Sergeants, three Corporals and 20 conscripts.
Line Personnel	27 Captains, 25 First Lieutenants, 48 Second Lieutenants, 11 Cadets, 28 First Sergeants, 117 Sergeants, 199 Corporals, 28 Cooks, 29 Cornets, 27 Private Barbers and 1,726 privates.

On 1 August 1947, by General Order the Army created the Presidential Guard a few weeks before the inauguration of the new government building, the National Palace, with the mission of guarding it and forming troops to render military honours at official events to heads of state and diplomats visiting the government house.

Territorially, the Army forces were organised into two Departments and the General Headquarters in the 1930s, distributed as shown in Table 2.[1]

Table 2: Dominican National Army Organisation in the 1930s

General Headquarters (Ciudad Trujillo)
General Staff
Generalissimo Trujillo Regiment
Ramfis Regiment
General Trujillo Teaching Centre
Trujillo City Post Command
Law & Intelligence Office
Weapons Quartermaster
Navy Quartermaster
Army Aviation Administration
Army Aviation Corps
Army Aviation Detachment
Army Corps of Engineers
Radiotelegraphy and Signals Detachment
Cavalry Squadron
Navy Detachment
Quartermaster Detachment
Artillery and Machine Gun Company
2nd, 7th, 15th, 17th, 21st, 22nd, 24th, 25th, Infantry Companies
Army Music Band
North Department (Santiago)
10th & 14th Infantry Companies (Santiago)
8th Infantry Company (Puerto Plata)
23rd Infantry Company (Monte Cristi)
19th Infantry Company (Monte Cristi)
3rd Infantry Company (La Vega)
6th Infantry Company (San Francisco de Macorís)
13th Infantry Company (Samaná)
18th Infantry Company (Moca)
South Department (San Cristóbal)
1st Infantry Company (San Pedro de Macorís)
5th Infantry Company (Barahona)
9th Infantry Company (Azua)
11th Infantry Company (Seybo)
12th Infantry Company (San Cristóbal)

In the mid-1960s the Dominican National Army was restructured into four brigades, namely:

- First Army Brigade: Its headquarters was in Santo Domingo (formerly Ciudad Trujillo), with three infantry battalions and an engineer-sapper battalion with 2,198 men. Its area of responsibility was Santo Domingo and the south-east of the island.
- Second Army Brigade: Its headquarters was in Santiago, with five infantry battalions with 2,482 men. Its area of responsibility was the centre and north-west of the island.
- Third Army Brigade: Its headquarters was in San Juan de la Maguana, with two infantry battalions with 1,285 men. It had territorial responsibility over the south-east and the Haitian border up to Monte Cristi.
- Fourth Army Brigade: This brigade was formed during the provisional government of Héctor García-Godoy, right after the civil war. Most of this officers, non-commissioned officers and troops, besides all armoured vehicles, tanks and artillery came from the dissolved CEFA (*Centro de Enseñanza de las Fuerzas Armadas*/Armed Forces Teaching Centre). Its headquarters was established in Santa Cruz de Mao.

This organisation was kept well into the 1970s.

The Commanders of the Dominican National Army were as shown in Table 3.[2]

Table 3: Commanders of the Dominican National Army 1928-1967

Officer	Service dates
Brigadier General Rafael Leónidas Trujillo	17 May 1928 to 17 August 1930
Brigadier General Simón Díaz	17 August 1930 to 15 July 1931
Brigadier General Ramón Vázquez Rivera	15 July 1931 to 07 May 1933
Brigadier General José García	07 May 1933 to 01 December 1934
Brigadier General Federico Fiallo	01 December 1934 to 01 November 1935
Brigadier General Aníbal Trujillo Molina	01 November 1935 to 02 November 1936
Brigadier General Héctor Bienvenido Trujillo	02 November 1936 to 01 January 1944
Brigadier General Fernando A. Sánchez	01 January 1944 to 12 July 1944
Brigadier General Federico Fiallo	12 July 1944 to 23 December 1946
Brigadier General Fausto E. Caamaño Medina	23 December 1946 to 03 April 1948
Brigadier General Fernando A. Sánchez	03 April 1948 to 01 May 1949
Brigadier General José García Trujillo	01 May 1949 to 03 February 1952
Brigadier General Ernesto Pérez González	05 June 1952 to 17 November 1953
Brigadier General Virgilio García Trujillo	17 November 1953 to 20 December 1954
Brigadier General Félix Hermida González	19 January 1955 to 16 July 1957
Brigadier General Virgilio García Trujillo	10 November 1957 to 18 November 1958
Brigadier General Santos Marte Pichardo (*)	18 November 1958 to 22 January 1959
Brigadier General Máximo R. Bonetti Burgos (*)	22 January 1959 to 16 July 1959
Brigadier General José R. Román Fernández	16 July 1959 to 02 August 1960
Brigadier General Fernando A. Sánchez Jr.	02 August 1960 to 16 July 1961
Brigadier General Virgilio García Trujillo	16 July 1961 to 19 November 1961

Officer	Service dates
Brigadier General Luis Román Tirado	19 November 1961 to 21 January 1962
Brigadier General Marcos A. Jorge Moreno	21 January 1962 to 17 July 1962
Brigadier General Marcos A. Rivera Cuesta	17 July 1962 to 19 January 1963
Brigadier General Renato Ungría Morel	19 January 1963 to 01 February 1964
Brigadier General Salvador A. Montás Guerrero	01 February 1964 to 17 February 1965
Brigadier General Juan M. Lora Fernández (+)	17 February 1965 to 18 May 1965
Brigadier General Marcos A. Rivera Cuesta (&)	17 February 1965 to 10 September 1965
Brigadier General Jacinto Martínez Arana	10 September 1965 to 06 January 1966
Brigadier General Enrique Pérez y Pérez	06 January 1966 to 26 February 1966
Brigadier General Elio O. Perdomo Rosario	26 February 1966 to 15 February 1967

(*) Interim Commander
(+) Constitutionalist Commander during the Civil War
(&) Loyalist Commander during the Civil War

Commanders of the Army between 1928 and 1967: Brigadier Generals Rafael Trujillo, Simón Díaz, Ramón Vásquez, José García, Federico Fiallo, Aníbal Trujillo, Héctor Trujillo, Fernando Sánchez, Fausto Caamaño, José García Trujillo, Ernesto Pérez, Virgilio García Trujillo, Félix Hermida, Santos Marte Pichardo, Máximo Bonetti, José Román, Fernando Sánchez, Luis Román, Jorge Moreno, Marcos Rivera, Renato Ungría, Salvador Montás, Juan María Lora, Jacinto Martínez, Enrique Pérez y Pérez and Elio Perdomo. (*Ejército Nacional Dominicano*).

An M3 Stuart light tank of the Dominican National Army during military manoeuvres in the 1950s (left). Four M3A1 armoured cars of the National Army (right). (*Ejército Nacional Dominicano*)

Military trucks and jeeps during a ceremony in the 1950s (left). The only two M3 Stuart light tanks in the Dominican National Army, which were later transferred to the AMD (right). (*Ejército Nacional Dominicano*)

Landsverk L-60L light tanks (top left), Landsverk Lynx armoured vehicles (top right), AMX-13/75 light tanks (bottom left) and M3A1 Stuart light tank with several M3 Half Track armoured vehicles. Although originally acquired for the National Army, they were all transferred to the AMD Armoured Battalion. After the civil war, they would return to the Army. (Luis Puesan and Albert Grandolini Archives)

Table 4: Dominican Army tanks and armoured vehicles[3]

Vehicle	Quantity	Year of acquisition
M3 Stuart light tank (*)	2	1943
M3A1 Scout car (*)	4	1943
M2 & M3 Half Track (*)	16	1948
M16/M3A1 Half Track with four .50 cal. Browning AAMGs (*)	4	1948
LTV-1 Alligator amphibious vehicle	20	1948
Landsverk L-60L light tank with a 37mm gun (+)	25	1956
Landsverk Lynx armoured vehicle (Pansarbil m/39) with a 20mm gun (+)	13	1956
AMX-13/75 light tank with a 75mm gun (+)	15	1960
(*) CEFA had all the tanks and military vehicles from 1959 to 1966. The FAD kept the two M3 Half Tracks with anti-aircraft guns since the other two were destroyed in 1965. (+) The L-60Ls, Lynx vehicles and AMX-13 tanks received AMD and later FAD markings.		

The best and most powerful artillery pieces were purchased for the CEFA, thus the Army relied on some First World War 75mm Schneider, Krupp and St. Chamond guns.

Between 1946 and 1948 Brazil exported armament to the Dominican Army as shown in Table 5.[4]

Table 5: Armament exported by Brazil to Dominican Republic

Quantity	Armament	Ammunition
12	75mm Saint Chamond guns	12,000 projectiles
Unknown	75mm Schneider M1919 guns	Unknown
4	105mm Krupp C14 guns	10,000 projectiles
8	75mm Krupp C14 guns	12,000 projectiles
12	75mm Krupp C28 guns	Unknown
10	37mm M3 antitank guns	12,500 HE M63 projectiles 12,500 AP M51 projectiles
100	2.36-in M9A1 bazookas	150,000 rockets
100	81mm M29 Brandt mortars	240,000 grenades
1,000	7.92mm Mauser M98 rifles	Unknown

After the reestablishment of diplomatic relations with the United States, the American government sent a Military Assistance Advisory Group (MAAG) to the Dominican Republic, with 13 members, who were responsible for training personnel of the Dominican Armed Forces in counterinsurgency tactics.

A platoon of the Dominican Army marching. The soldiers carry Mauser rifles (top). Practice with 37mm M3 anti-tank guns (bottom). The regular daily uniform was khaki with the M1 helmet in olive green. (Albert Grandolini Archives)

Soldiers of the Dominican National Army practicing shooting with San Cristóbal carbines manufactured in the country (left). Two soldiers with an 81mm M29 Brandt mortar (right). (Albert Grandolini Archives)

Within the Army, there were three elite units, each with 800 men, all of them near the capital:

- *Juan Pablo Duarte* Battalion: based at *16 de Agosto* Military Camp, on Duarte Highway, 17 miles from the capital.
- *Francisco del Rosario* Battalion: stationed at *27 de Febrero* Military Camp also on Duarte Highway, which linked Santo Domingo with Santiago, about four miles from the capital.
- *Ramón Mella* Battalion: garrisoned at San Cristóbal, around 18 miles from the capital.

All three battalions were equipped the light and heavy machine guns and bazookas. There was also an Artillery Battalion very close to *27 de Febrero* Military Camp on Duarte Highway, with 250 men, with cannons, howitzers and mortars.

Within the capital, there were four Army units:

- The Transportation Battalion: Located in the north part of Santo Domingo, with 350 personnel, mainly mechanics and drivers.
- The Army Quartermaster: It had around 200 men, mostly bureaucrats, and it was located near the Transportation Battalion.
- The War Material Depot: a huge warehouse which stored explosives, grenades, ammunition and bazookas, with 175 personnel.
- The Presidential Guard: Located near the Presidential Palace, with between 450 and 500 well-armed men.

Armed Forces Training Centre (*Centro de Entrenamiento de las Fuerzas Armadas*/CEFA)

This quasi-independent organisation within the armed forces, originally established by Ramfis Trujillo, on 5 June 1959, to protect the government. It was an elite force whose headquarters was at San Isidro Air Base and was composed of:

- *General Gregorio Luperón* Artillery Battalion, with recoilless rifles (Swedish Bofors) and several pieces of artillery.
- *27 de Febrero* Armoured Battalion, which was equipped with tanks and armoured vehicles (See Table 4 above).
- Three infantry battalions, with 2,834 well-armed men.

Dominican Air Force (*Fuerza* Aérea Dominicana/FAD)

In 1932, the Dominican government officially created the Military Air Arm through Decree No. 297, attached to the National Army. On 26 October 1942 it was named the Aviation Company of the National Army. Then, on 2 January 1948, President Trujillo signed the Decree No. 4,910 through which the Dominican Military Aviation (*Aviación Militar Dominicana*/AMD) was created, establishing its General Staff and the total independence of the National Army. In the short period from 1955 to 1957, the AMD was called the Dominican Air Force, but then it returned to its previous name. It was only on 9 February 1962 that the Dominican government issued Decree No. 7,222 by which the Dominican Military Aviation was definitively renamed as the Dominican Air Force (*Fuerza* Aérea Dominicana/FAD). Its present name is Dominican Republic Air Force (*Fuerza* Aérea de República Dominicana/FARD).

In the years of the Second World War, the Dominican Republic also benefited from American aircraft through the Lend-Lease Program of the US government, although on a smaller scale compared to other countries. Thus, they received three Boeing-Stearman PT-17 Kaydets, three North American AT-6C Texans, five Vultee BT-13A Valiants, three Aeronca L-3B Grasshoppers and one Piper AE-1 (L-4) in 1943. In 1944 they received three PT 17s and three AT-6Ds. The Dominican government had acquired four Piper J-5A Cubs in 1941 for basic training.

After the Second World War, the Dominican Military Aviation acquired two unarmed B-17G bombers from civil sources in Canada, which were armed in the Dominican Republic in 1947. Then, the AMD acquired its first two PBY-5A Catalina and its first fighters, 11 Lockheed P-38 Lightning, including four P-38Ls, two P-38Ms and five F-5Gs between 1947 and 1948. If the Cayo Confites Expedition had been carried out in 1947, P-38s of the *Fuerza Aérea del Ejército de la Revolución Americana* (Air Force of the American Revolution Army, FAERA) would have fought against AMD P-38s.[5] That year,

Large number of Vultee BT-13 basic trainers at San Isidro Air Base in the late 1940s. In the background, the two B-17s and a C-46 can be seen (top). North American AT-6C Texan advanced trainers of the Dominican Military Aviation (bottom). (FAD).

the AMD bought 12 North American T-6C/D Texans from a private company in Florida, and also three Curtiss C-46A Commandos from Canada. At least three Beech UC-45F and an AT-11 were also acquired in the late 1940s for the AMD. In 1948, the AMD started acquiring P-51 Mustang fighters, the first being a P-51C. That year, another five Mustangs, a P-51A, a P-51C and three P-51Ds (one of the latter an F-6D) were purchased, all of them from civil sources and without any guns, which were installed in the Dominican Republic.

After the end of the US Military Mission in the Dominican Republic, President Trujillo decided to hire at least 10 American instructors to continue training AMD pilots. In addition to them, a former Luftwaffe pilot, Major Otto Hans Winterer was also hired and subsequently eight former military pilots from Brazil with two aeronautical engineers and three aviation mechanics of the same nationality.

On 15 February 1948, through Decree Nr. 4918, the Military Air Arm was renamed Military Aviation Corps, completely independent from the Army, with its own commander and chief of staff. In that year, the AMD wanted to acquire Avro Lancaster heavy bombers and Supermarine Spitfire fighters from Great Britain, but in the end five de Havilland Mosquito FB.Mk 6 fighter-bombers and 10 Bristol Beaufighter TF.Mk 10 fighter-bombers were purchased, with a good number of 116-pound conventional bombs, 60-pound unguided rockets and 20mm and 7.62mm ammunition for the cannons and machine guns of the above-mentioned aircraft. By the end of the 1950s, all British flying equipment was already withdrawn from service. In 1949, two Hiller UH-12 helicopters were acquired and also three North American B-25H/J Mitchell medium bombers, which arrived in the country in 1950. Later a B-25C was also purchased. In 1951, four PBY-6A and two OA-10A Catalinas were

In the late 1940s, the AMD acquired its first fighters, Lockheed P-38 Lightnings (left) and the North American P-51 Mustangs (right). (Kendall W. Everson & Robert Serrata)

AMD Mustangs and Lightnings fighters. From left to right: A P-38L, an F-5G, a P-38M, an early P-51D, in this case painted in overall black, and a rare P-51A. (Randy Haskins via Albert Grandolini)

The only two heavy bombers in AMD service were a pair of B-17G Flying Fortresses acquired after the Second World War. (Albert Grandolini Archives)

A unique feature of the Dominican Military Aviation was the incorporation of de Havilland Mosquito (left) and Bristol Beaufighter (right) heavy fighters in the late 1940s. (Luis de León and Peter Amos via Albert Grandolini)

acquired, which were later transferred to the Naval Aviation. In 1952, a B-25G was purchased, also a De Havilland Canada DHC-2 Beaver and four Cessna T-50 Bobcats.

The first combat operation of the new AMD took place on 14 June 1949, when a flight consisting of a Beaufighter fighter-bomber and two Mosquitoes attacked a Catalina amphibious plane and two Dominican exile boats in Luperón Bay. The rebels managed to deploy 14 aircraft to support their invasion, but their forces were quickly captured by the National Army without fighting, all of them but five being executed. A PBY Catalina was destroyed by AMD aircraft and its American crew captured and executed.

In the 1950s, the AMD was reorganised, creating the Fighter & Training Squadron, with two sections, one for fighters and another for the Aviation School, and the Bomber Squadron. In addition, there was a Naval Patrol Section and a Transportation Section. In 1952 the name of the Fighter & Training Squadron was changed into the *Ramfis* Fighter Squadron, in honour of Trujillo's son, Colonel Ramfis Trujillo, who was the AMD Deputy Chief of Staff. On 4 June 1953, Colonel Rafael Leónidas Trujillo Jr (Ramfis) was appointed Commander of the AMD. He was only 23 years old at that time, and only six months later he was promoted to Brigadier General, the youngest General in Dominican history. In 1953, he was promoted again, this time to Major General.

In 1952, the Military Aviation wanted to acquire Supermarine Seafire Mk. XV and Spitfire Mk. XXII fighters but instead and under the Reimbursable Air Program (RAP) of the American government, the AMD received 25 Republic P-47D-30-RA Thunderbolt fighters which were assigned to a new Fighter-Bomber Squadron called *Leónidas*, in honour of President Trujillo's middle name. Due to the acquisition of P-51Ds and Vampire jets from the Swedish Air Force, the P-47Ds were in active service only for a few years. It was also in 1952 that 32 North American P-51D Mustang fighters were acquired from Sweden and 10 more in 1953. In 1954 a TF-51K, an advanced trainer for the Mustang fighters, was bought. Also in the 1950s, the first Douglas C-47Bs and a C-54 Skymaster were acquired for the Transport Squadron of the AMD. Swedish maintenance personnel were hired to train their Dominican counterparts in handling the Mustangs and Vampires. Trujillo had hired some retired Brazilian military pilots to train AMD pilots in the 1950s and later some USAF instructors came to the Dominican Republic. On 22 March 1953, San Isidro Air Force Base (AFB) was officially inaugurated.

Between 1953 and 1958 the acquisition of T-6 Texans also increased significantly. In 1954, 40 Texans were purchased, adding to the 25 that operated at AMD. Most were used for training pilots, although many of them were armed and could carry bombs or rockets. In 1954, the American government, through its military mission in the Dominican Republic, offered a package of 25 North American F-86F-30-NA Sabre fighters and four Lockheed T-33A Shooting Stars for the AMD, in order to replace the P-47s and P-51s. They then changed the F-86s to F-84 Thunderjets, which was not accepted by the AMD. It was then that an attempt was made to acquire British aircraft, Supermarine Attacker FB.2 fighter-bombers, Gloster Meteor F.8 fighters and T.7 advanced trainers, which although the sale was approved by the United Kingdom authorities, did not come to fruition, because Sweden once again offered fighters at more affordable prices. Thus, 25 De Havilland DH100 Vampire F.Mk 1 fighters were acquired, with a sufficient quantity of 20mm ammunition for their guns, a large stock of spare parts and two reserve turbines for $75,000. These jets had been built under license by SAAB of Sweden under the name Vampire J.28A.

A peculiar aspect of the AMD was that in the mid-1950s, it obtained its own infantry troops, armoured vehicles and artillery, in open competition with the Army. The AMD soldiers used the German *Stahlhem* Model 1942 helmet, which they had purchased from Spain. The 25 Landverk L60/m40 light tanks, 13 Landverk m/39 Lynx assault vehicles and 20 105mm Bofors Infanterikannon m/45 recoilless anti-armour guns, all Swedish material acquired with the Vampires, were assigned to the AMD Armoured Battalion but were later transferred to the Army. Besides, the AMD also had an Artillery Battalion with 12 Spanish 105mm Reinosa 105/26 howitzers, 24 Spanish 120mm ECIA mortars and four 20mm Hispano-Suiza 804 DCA anti-aircraft guns.

Ramfis Trujillo, the dictator's spoiled son, became at the age of 23 the youngest Major General in Dominican history and more than an officer, he was a playboy. He was Commander of the FAD between 1952 and 1958 and an FAD fighter squadron bore his name. (Public Domain)

The Republic P-47D Thunderbolt fighters of the *Leónidas* Fighter-Bomber Squadron had a short operational life in the FAD of only five years. (Dax Roman & Luis de León)

The *Ramfis* Fighter Squadron had for sure the most colourful and heavily decorated Mustangs in service in the FAD in the 1950s. Later they adopted a simpler colour scheme. (Lennard Engerby & FAD)

In the 1950s, AMD acquired dozens of North American T-6 Texans, which were armed and could carry bombs. At least 70 Texans were in service with the AMD/FAD. (Luis de León)

One of the AMD's four Lockheed T-33As that were in service for less than two years. (Rafael Martí via Albert Grandolini)

Military Aviation infantry troops wearing the traditional khaki uniform and the German *Stahlhem* Model 1942 helmet. These elite troops were better armed than those of the Army. (Luis Puesan). Below, a soldier with a Spanish CETME A1 assault rifle. (Albert Grandolini Archives)

Two De Havilland DH100 Vampire F.Mk 1 fighters of the AMD at San Isidro Air Base in the mid-1950s. In the background 10 P-47D fighters, four Curtiss C-46s, a Douglas B-26B, a Lockheed Lodestar and a PBY-5A Catalina can be seen. (FAD)

The two types of De Havilland DH100 Vampire fighters acquired by the AMD from Sweden: F.Mk 1s (top) and FB.Mk 50s (bottom) at San Isidro Air Base in the 1950s. (Albert Grandolini Archives)

Some helicopter types used by AMD/FAD: From left to right, Hiller UH-12, Sikorsky S.55C and Sud Aviation Alouette 2. (Albert Grandolini Archives)

One Douglas C-47 (left) and three Curtiss C-46s (right) of the FAD Transport Squadron. (Dick Lohuis & FAD)

In 1957, the AMD received four Lockheed T-33A jets from the United States, and they were used as advanced jet trainers. The same year 17 more Vampire fighter jets were purchased from Sweden; these were de Havilland Vampire FB.Mk 50s, known in the Swedish Air Force as J.28Bs. These fighters were in service until 1974. Since the AMD wanted more T-33As for advanced training and the US was not willing to deliver them, an attempt was made to purchase 12 BAC Jet Provost trainers, but to no avail. Also in 1957, two Sikorsky S.55C helicopters were acquired for *Dominicana de Aviación* airlines but transferred to the AMD and a third example was added in 1959. That year, the AMD purchased seven demilitarised Douglas B-26Bs, which were armed in the Dominican Republic for the Bomber Squadron but also used for transport duties.

In August 1958, two AMD Vampire F.Mk 1 fighters intercepted a US Navy Grumman Albatross near the town of Cabrera. The latter was flying from Guantánamo, Cuba to Puerto Rico and was forced to land at Santiago AFB. In December of the same year, two AMD P-51Ds and a Vampire FB.Mk 50 intercepted a Brazilian Air Force Lockheed P2V-5 Neptune, which was on a ferry flight from the US to Brazil. It was forced to land at Trujillo AFB and after being inspected by the AMD it was allowed to continue its flight to Brazil.

During the fight against the guerrilla of the *Movimiento de Liberación Dominicano* (Dominican Liberation Movement) in 1959, P-51D and Vampire fighters and armed T-6D Texans were deployed to the Constanza area, and also around 1,200 Army effectives. During the month of July, while the Mustangs and Vampires attacked the rebel vessels on the coast with rockets, the Texan strafed and bombed the guerrillas inland. Due to poor weather conditions, at least five Vampires and a Texan were lost in accidents during this campaign, and two pilots being killed. The guerrilla organisation was completely eliminated.

On 1 October 1959, the First Parachute Company of the AMD was created, which had 120 troops. These elite troops were armed with Spanish 7.62mm CETME Model B and Belgian FN FAL assault rifles.

Two medium bombers that were in service in the FAD: North American B-25J Mitchell (left) and Douglas B-26B Invader (right). (Gary Fitton & Rafael Martí via Albert Grandolini)

Personnel of the First Parachute Company of the AMD in 1959. From left to right, 2nd Lieutenants Salvador Lluberes Montás, Isidoro Martínez, Freddy Franco Díaz and José Antonio Rosario Espinal, with a Spanish Army instructor (centre). (FAD)

Mustangs Versus Thunderbolts

The Republic P-47 Thunderbolt fighters were active in the FAD for only five years, but during that time there was great rivalry between the pilots of these fighters and those of the P-51 Mustangs.

The P-47s were part of the *Leónidas* Fighter-Bomber Squadron and was organised into five flights of four aircraft each, which were identified with the colours red, yellow, orange, green and blue. Later, given the operational losses, four flights were established with the letters A, B, C and D. By the end of the 1950s, the P-47s were retired when the de Havilland Vampire jet fighters were acquired from Sweden.

The P-51 Mustang fighters were part of the *Ramfis* Fighter Squadron and were organised into flights of five aircraft that were identified with the colours black, red, yellow and blue, with the numbers 1, 2, 3, and 4 indicating their flight. They serviced in the FAD for decades, being withdrawn from service in 1984.

P-51 and P-47 fighters share the ramp at the Santiago de los Caballeros Air Base in 1955. (Luis de León)

Pilots of the P-51D Mustang (top) and P-47D Thunderbolt (bottom) fighters, whose rivalry lasted for much of the 1950s. (FAD)

AMD Republic P-47D Thunderbolt fighters of the *Leónidas* Fighter-Bomber Squadron in the mid-1950s. (FAD)

The first Swedish technicians to arrive in the Dominican Republic to serve with the AMD in 1954. From left to right: Ove Helderud, Curt Stodberg, Folke Gardvall, Valter Ekberg, Yngve Humble, Bennet Pettersson, Harje Kjellberg and Lennart Engerby (left). Pilots of the fighter-bomber Squadron in 1958: standing, from left to right, 2nd Lieutenants Vinicio Morales Bobadilla and Nicanor Acosta Paulino, 1st Lieutenant José Alberto Martínez Rincón, 2nd Lieutenant Alfredo Alcibiades Hernández Díaz, 1st Lieutenant Marino Polanco Tovar and 2nd Lieutenant Pedro Héctor Dipp Medina. Kneeling, from left to right: Captains Ismael Emilio Román Carbuccia and Federico Ismael Fernández Smester, 2nd Lieutenant Ramón Napoleón Rojas Nolasco and 1st Lieutenant Arístides Ramírez Gómez (right). (Lennart Engerby & FAD)

A fighter pilot from the *Ramfis* Squadron proudly poses next to his P-51 Mustang in the mid-1950s. (FAD)

Table 6: Dominican Air Force aircraft from the late 1940s to the mid-1960s[6]

Aircraft	Quantity	Role
De Havilland DH100 Vampire FB.Mk 50 (J.28B)	17	Fighter-bomber
De Havilland DH100 Vampire F.Mk 1 (J.28A)	25	Fighter
Lockheed AT-33A Shooting Star	4	Advanced trainer
North American P-51A/C/D/TF-51D/F-6K Mustang (+)	1/2/45/1/1	Fighter/advanced trainer
Republic P-47D-30-RA Thunderbolt	25	Fighter/fighter-bomber
Lockheed P-38L/M/F-5G Lightning	4/2/5	Fighter/ Photoreconnaissance
De Havilland DH98 Mosquito FB.Mk 6	5	Fighter-bomber
De Havilland DH98 Mosquito T.Mk 29	3	Fighter-bomber/advanced trainer
Bristol Beaufighter TF.Mk 10 (Mk.VIF)	10	Fighter-bomber
Vega/Douglas B-17G Flying Fortress	1/1	Heavy bomber
North American B-25C/ G/H/J Mitchell	1/1/1/2	Medium bomber/transport
Douglas B-26B Invader	7	Medium bomber/transport
Lockheed B-34 Ventura	1	Medium bomber
Lockheed PV-1 Ventura	2	Medium bomber/sea patrol
Boeing-Stearman PT-13/ PT-17 Kaydet	32	Primary trainer
Piper J5A Cub	4	Primary trainer/liaison
Vultee BT-13A Valiant	21	Basic trainer
North American AT-6C/T-6D/SNJ-3/4 Texan	70	Advanced trainer/light attack
North American T-28A/D Trojan	3/6	Advanced trainer
Consolidated PBY-5A/ PBY-6A Catalina (*)	2/4	Sea Patrol
Canadian Vickers OA-10A Catalina (*)	2	Sea Patrol
Douglas C-54 Skymaster	3	Transport
Douglas C-47B	7	Transport
Curtiss C-46A Commando	5	Transport
Beechcraft UC-45F/C-45H Expeditor	7/1	Transport
Beechcraft AT-11 Kansan	2	Light bomber/bomber trainer
Lockheed C-60 Lodestar	1	Transport
Aero Commander 520	1	VIP transport
De Havilland Canada DHC-2 Beaver	1	Light transport
Republic RC-3 Seabee (*)	1	Light transport
Cessna T-50/UC-78 Bobcat	4	Transport trainer/light transport
Aeronca L-3B Grasshopper	3	Light transport/liaison
Piper AE-1 (L-4)	1	Liaison/Air ambulance
North American NA-145 Navion	1	Liaison/light transport
Stinson 108 Voyager	1	VIP transport
Cessna 170	1	Liaison/light transport
Cessna 180	1	Light transport
Cessna U-17A	1	Light transport
Hiller UH-12B/C Raven	1/1	Utility helicopter
Sikorsky S.55C/H-19	2/1	Utility helicopter/SAR
Sud Aviation SA313E Alouette 2	2	Utility helicopter/SAR
Sud Aviation SA319B Alouette 3	1	Utility helicopter/SAR

(*) Transferred to the Dominican Naval Aviation. (+) Between 1963 and 1965 12 P-51Ds were completely refurbished by Trans-Florida Aviation (later Cavalier) with new engines, propellers and communication systems.

The Pilots' Rebellion

The return of Héctor and José Trujillo to Santo Domingo on 15 November 1961 incensed US President John F. Kennedy, who dispatched a US Navy fleet of 14 vessels with Marine troops, including two aircraft carriers with fighter jets to Dominican waters. This was done to push both Trujillo brothers and their nephew Ramfis out of the country. In the meantime, the so-called Pilots' Rebellion took place, which started in the morning of 19 November.

The artillery and tank squadron of San Isidro Air Base were bombed by two FAD P-51 Mustang fighters who had taken off from Santiago AFB under the orders of the Commander of that base General Pedro Rafael Rodríguez Echavarría. There were also 11 Vampire fighters that took off from Santiago AFB bound to Santo Domingo, divided in two groups, one led by Major González Pomares and the other by Major Ramírez Gómez. They were all armed with HVAR rockets. The bombs and rockets did not affect the buildings since they were aimed nearby just to frighten the CEFA personnel. Two other Mustangs attacked the Army artillery garrison at Villa Mella and the Army Headquarters, causing very little damage. In the afternoon of that day, the Vampires also attacked other military installations that remained loyal to Trujillo such as the Mao and Puerto Plata Army Garrisons. These attacks managed to dissuade the military forces that supported the Trujillos and achieved the definitive departure of the Trujillo remnants from the country.

This uprising prevented *Petán* and *Negro* Trujillo from executing a plot to dethrone Joaquín Balaguer from the presidency of the Republic and assassinate the main leaders of the National Civic Union (UCN) and the 14 of June Movement. On the night of 18 November, the then head of the Air Force, Mayor General Virgilio García Trujillo, the head of the Army Mayor General Fernando *Tunti* Sánchez Jr, and the regional head of the feared SIM in Santiago, Alicinio Peña Rivera, had met at San Isidro Air Base with *Petán* Trujillo. They were planning the assassination of some political leaders such as Viriato Fiallo and Joaquín Balaguer, among others. This plan was called *Operación Luz Verde* (Operation Green Light) or the San Bartolomé Massacre. But this plan was leaked and aborted by the FAD officers Lieutenant Colonels Manuel Durán Guzmán, Raymundo Polanco Alegría, Commander of the *Ramfis* Fighter Squadron, and Nelton González Pomares, Commander of the Fighter-Bomber Squadron. They were led by Brigadier General Pedro Rafael Rodríguez Echavarría, at that time Commander of the Santiago Air Base, and Colonels Pedro Santiago *Chaguito* Rodríguez Echavarría and Federico Fernández Smester.

The plot prevented José Arismendy (*Petán*) and Héctor Bienvenido (*Negro*) Trujillo Molina from returning to power and reviving the regime headed by Rafael Leónidas Trujillo, and it meant the definitive departure of the Trujillos from the Dominican Republic.

Organisation of the FAD

As previously mentioned, in 1962 the AMD changed its name to Dominican Air Force (*Fuerza* Aérea Dominicana/FAD). In 1963, the FAD was organised as follows:

- Headquarters and Chief of Staff: located at San Isidro Air Base in near Santo Domingo. It also included a headquarters company.
- *Escuadrón de Combate "Dragones"* (Combat Squadron Dragon): This squadron was formed in 1961 with the merger of three squadrons:
  Escuadrón de Caza-Bombardero (Fighter-Bomber Squadron): Its complement of combat aircraft included 34 Vampire F.Mk 1/FB.Mk 50s, one B-25C, one B-25G, two B-25Hs, one B-25J and six T-6D Texans. This was the former *Leónidas* Fighter-Bomber Squadron.
  Escuadrón de Caza (Fighter Squadron): Its complement of combat aircraft included 31 F-51 Mustangs and 12 T-6D Texans. This was the former *Ramfis* Fighter Squadron.
  Escuadrón de Reconocimiento (Reconnaissance Squadron): It had a fleet of seven B-26B Invaders and six T-6Ds.
  Its headquarters was San Isidro Air Base near Santo Domingo. All combat aircraft had their firing range on Catalina Island.
- *Escuadrón de Transporte Aéreo "Pegasus"* (Pegasus Air Transport Squadron): Its fleet included five C-46s, five C-47s, three C-54s, a C-60, two C-45s, two AT-11s, an AC 520, three Cessna 170s and a U-17A. This squadron was created on 19 May 1958. Its headquarters was in San Isidro Air Base near Santo Domingo.
- *Escuadrón de Rescate "Aguilas"* (Eagles Rescue Squadron): It brought together the few helicopters in service at the time, including three Hiller UH-12s, three Sikorsky S-55Cs, two Alouette 2s and an Alouette 3. Its headquarters was also in San Isidro Air Base near Santo Domingo.
- *Escuela de Aviación Militar* (Military Aviation School): The Training Squadron had 15 T-6C/Ds, three T-28As and six T-28Ds. Its headquarters was in San Isidro Air Base near Santo Domingo.
- *Escuadrón de Mantenimiento* (Maintenance Squadron), also in San Isidro Air Base
- FAD Infantry Battalion: This battalion included three infantry companies and a support armoured company, the latter with 25 Landsverk L-60L light tanks, 13 Landsverk Lynx armoured vehicles (Pansarbil m/39) and 15 AMX-13/75 light tanks
- Base Operations company
- FAD General Quartermaster, with one company
- FAD Health Service

Total Aircraft in service in 1963: 157
Total FAD personnel: 1,538 men, including 151 officers, 36 cadets, and 1,351 non-commissioned officers and troops.

The FAD Training Squadron of the Military Aviation School had T-28A/D Trojans and T-6C/D Texans for advanced training. (Dick Lohuis via Albert Grandolini and FAD)

A group of cadets from the Military Aviation School posing with their flight suits in front of the flight line of the T-6 advanced trainers. (Albert Grandolini Archives)

AMD Maintenance Squadron at San Isidro AFB in 1959. AMD technicians pose with their Swedish counterparts next to a *Ramfis* Squadron P-51D Mustang (left). Some de Havilland Vampire F.Mk 1s inside the maintenance hangar at San Isidro AFB in the 1950s (right). (FAD)

Table 7: Commanders of the AMD/FAD 1948-1967[7]

Officer	Service dates
Colonel Fernando Manuel Castillo (*)	15 February 1948 to 28 June 1949
Lieutenant General Federico Fiallo	28 June 1949 to 11 June 1950
Brigadier General Frank A. Feliz Miranda (*)	11 June 1950 to 16 January 1951
Brigadier General Félix Hermida	16 January 1951 to 04 June 1952
Mayor General Rafael Leónidas Trujillo (Ramfis)	04 June 1952 to 28 August 1958
Mayor General Fernando Sánchez Jr.	28 August 1958 to 01 June 1960
Mayor General Virgilio García Trujillo	01 June 1960 to 16 July 1961
Mayor General Fernando Sánchez Jr.	16 July 1961 to 19 November 1961
Major General Félix Hermida	19 November 1961 to 22 November 1961
Brigadier General Pedro S. Rodríguez Echavarría (*)	22 November 1961 to 19 January 1962
Brigadier General Miguel Atila Luna Pérez (*)	19 January 1962 to 23 January 1964
Brigadier General Ismael Emilio Román Carbucia (*)	23 January 1964 to 18 January 1965
Brigadier General Juan de los Santos Céspedes (*)	18 January 1965 to 26 February 1966
Brigadier General Juan N. Folch Pérez (*)	26 February 1966 to 17 September 1966
Brigadier General Antonio Álvarez Albizu (*)	17 September 1966 to 06 September 1967
(*) Pilots.	

FAD Serial System

In 1950, four-digit serials were adopted. Aircraft and helicopters were given four digital series in one of these three blocks:

- 1000 for fighters and advanced trainers.
- 2000 for bombers and fighter-bombers.
- 3000 for other types including helicopters, transport aircraft and also advanced trainers.
- The first two digits signified the type of aircraft, followed by two sequential digits:

AMD/FAD Commanders between 1948 and 1967. Top row, from left to right: Colonel Fernando Castillo, Lieutenant Generals Federico Fiallo and Frank Feliz Miranda, Major Generals Félix Hermida, Ramfis Trujillo, Fernando Sánchez and Virgilio García. Bottom row, from left to right: Brig. Generals Félix Hermida, Pedro Rodríguez, Atila Luna, Emilio Román, Juan de los Santos Céspedes, Juan Folch and Antonio Álvarez. (FAD)

Table 8: FAD Serial System[8]

First two digits	Aircraft type
10	North American AT-6 Texan
11	Republic F-47D Thunderbolt
12	Vultee BT-13A Valiant
13	Boeing-Stearman PT-13/PT-17 Kaydet
14	Cessna UC-78/T-50 Bobcat
15	Beechcraft C-45/AT-11
19	North American F-51D Mustang
21	De Havilland Mosquito
23	Boeing B-17G Flying Fortress
24	Bristol Beaufighter
25	North American B-25 Mitchell
27	De Havilland Vampire
28	North American T-28A/D Trojan
29	Consolidated PBY-5A/PBY-6A Catalina, OA-10A Catalina
30	All helicopter types
31	Curtiss C-46 Commando
32	Douglas B-26 Invader (transport version)
33	Lockheed T-33A Shooting Star
34	Douglas C-47 Skytrain

The FAD had three main bases:

- *19 de Noviembre* AFB: located in San Isidro, around nine miles north-east of Santo Domingo. It was the FAD Headquarters and it had the main concentration of combat and transport aircraft, with around 2,000 men.
- *Coronel Piloto Juan Antonio Minaya Fernández* AFB: located at Santiago de los Caballeros. This unit was formed as *Zona Norte* (Northern Zone) on 26 June 1959 to control air operations in the north of the country. A few combat and transport aircraft were based there, with one battalion and a CEFA armoured platoon with some tanks and armoured vehicles.
- *Capitán Piloto Rafael A. Dávila Quezada* AFB: located in the city of Barahona, with some fighters, around 350 men and also a CEFA armoured detachment with some tanks and armoured vehicles.

There were also seven auxiliary air bases for rapid deployment in Montecristi, Puerto Plata, La Vega, Pedernales, Azua, San Cristóbal and La Romana. By 1965, the FAD had a total of 2,700 men including officers, NCOs and troops.

Dominican War Navy (*Marina de Guerra Dominicana*)

The Dominican Navy has remained active since 15 April 1844, participating in the process of the country's independence, civil wars and revolutions and many times clashing with its Haitian counterpart during the nineteenth century.

On 15 January 1934, the US Navy wooden-hulled Coast Guard cutters GC-1 and GC-2 arrived in the country, followed later by the Coast Guard cutter GC-3, also made of wood. These units were used by the American Navy to pursue liquor smugglers, and when the famous Prohibition Law was repealed, they were taken out of service and sold to the Dominican government. They were the first modern ships of the Dominican Navy.

In 1937, the equivalence of ranks between the officers of the Navy and the National Army was established, through General Order No. 93, of 14 July 1937, of the Commander in Chief of the National Army, and on 2 February 1938, General Order No. 11, established 17 Officers and 86 Enlisted Members as the authorised force of the National Navy.

On 10 April 1943, the National Navy Command was created and its Commander was Major Manuel A. Perdomo, who had been the assistant of Colonel McLaughlin, and directed it until 1947. In September 1943, construction work on the current *27 de Febrero* Naval Base began, in charge of an American Naval Assistance Mission under the orders of Commander Hilton, of the Coast Guard, a mission that was sent to the country because the Americans feared that Trujillo would maintain a pro-Hitler position during the Second World War. This base was inaugurated in 1944, but it remained under the control of the Army since most of the naval officers were taking training courses in the United States, from where they returned with three submarine chasers donated by the United States, commanded by Lieutenants Didiez Burgos, Rafael Arvelo and César de Windt Lavandier. As a result of this mission, in May 1944 the Navy School was opened at the Las Calderas Naval Base, under the direction of Commander Ramón Didiez Burgos.

By Decree No. 4169 of 10 February 1947, the Executive Branch ordered the organisation of the Navy with its own General Staff, designating the then Frigate Captain Ramón Didiez Burgos as its head. Then, the National Navy Command, directed by Major Manuel R. Perdomo, operated the Las Calderas Naval Base, the Beata Island Post. The Navy vessels included 10 Coast Guard cutters, three Auxiliary Boats, a Training Schooner, a Frigate and a Corvette with

The FAD two main bases, San Isidro AFB near Santo Domingo (left) and the Northern Command at Santiago de los Caballeros AFB (right). (FAD)

a Naval Corps staff that included 322 effectives. On 24 February of the same year, Lieutenant César De Windt Lavandier was promoted to the rank of Ship Captain and appointed Undersecretary of State for the Navy.

During 1948, Royal Navy Commander Sir John Agnew was brought to the country from Britain, along with other technicians from various specialties, to once again restructure the Naval Academy's teaching program. In that same year, the headquarters of the Navy Chief of Staff was moved three times: on 22 January, it was moved to the facilities where the Navy Liaison office operated, in Santo Domingo; On 22 May, it was installed in the building of the business Lockie y Cía, in the capital's port, and finally on 4 December in the then recently inaugurated Naval Base of Santo Domingo, which had been used to house troops of the National Army since its inauguration in 1947.

In 1949, the Executive Branch, by Decree No. 5713 of 23 March of that year, appointed Captain César De Windt Lavandier as Chief of Staff, replacing Frigate Captain Ramón Julio Didiez Burgos. On 16 April 1953, Captain Ramón Julio Didiez Burgos replaced Rear Admiral César De Windt Lavandier in the Navy Chief of Staff, who was appointed Naval Consultant to the President of the Republic. Didiez Burgos was replaced on 1 August of the same year by Brigadier General of the National Army José García Trujillo, who held the position for 16 days, since he was relieved on 16 August 1953 by Lieutenant Commander Luis Homero Lajara Burgos, appointed Chief of Staff of the institution with the temporary rank of Rear Admiral.

By 1950 the Dominican Navy had become the most powerful in the Caribbean. Its staff was 3,000 effectives, including officers, NCOs and troops, with a battalion of marines. Naval capacity remained relatively constant until the time after 1965 when larger ships were not replaced, and naval inventory steadily declined.

In March 1957, the San Cristóbal Naval Training Centre was created, based in the city of the same name. The *24 de Octubre* Naval Academy and the Naval Training Section were moved to the centre, which operated there until 10 November 1957, when it was transferred to the Las Calderas Naval Base. The other naval base was in Haina.

On 2 August 1958, the headquarters of the Naval Command and its offices were moved to the armed forces pavilion, located in the 'Heroes Centre'. In 1965, the personnel and units of the Navy participated in the civil war that broke out in the country starting on 24 April of that year, but when the rebellion of the units of the National Army against the triumvirate began, the Navy adopted

Four Frigates of the Dominican Navy. On the left, from top to bottom, F-101 ARD *Presidente Trujillo*, later *Mella*; F-102 ARD *Juan Pablo Duarte* and F-103 ARD *Presidente Troncoso* later *Gregorio Luperón*. On the right, the Frigate F-104 ARD *Presidente Peynado*, later *Cap. Gen. Pedro Santana*. (*Armada de República Dominicana* via Albert Grandolini)

The destroyers D-101 ARD *Trujillo*, later *Duarte* and D-102 ARD *Generalisimo*, later *Sánchez*, and the corvette C-101 ARD *Cristóbal Colón* of the Dominican Navy. (*Armada de República Dominicana*)

a neutral position. Once hostilities began between the troops of the Army and the Air Force on the one hand, and the Forces of the Constitutionalist Movement, among whom were Francisco Alberto Caamaño, at that time assigned to the FAD but with any relevant post, Manuel Montes Arache and other Navy officers, Commodore Francisco Javier Caminero moved within hours on the night of 26 April to the National Palace in the company of several officials, to assess the situation there and meet with President Dr. Rafael Molina Ureña. After leaving the government house, Commodore Rivera Caminero established contact with the General Staff and the ship commanders whom he informed about the visit. From that moment on, it abandoned its neutrality and it was then that the higher naval command ordered to shoot at the National Palace with naval guns, around noon on 27 April, an action that was carried out by several naval units stationed in the vicinity.

As a result of the *coup d'état* against the triumvirate and the events unleashed from that event, the Headquarters and General Staff of the Navy were installed aboard the frigate *Mella*, and on 8 May 1965, Commodore Rivera Caminero was appointed Minister of Defence.

Patrol Boat P-106 ARD *Libertad* of the Dominican Navy. (*Armada de República Dominicana*)

Dominican Navy LSM BA-104 ARD *Sirio* carrying some AMX-13/75 tanks on board during the 1963 crisis with Haiti. (Albert Grandolini Archives)

Table 9: Dominican War Navy ships 1945-1965[9]

Type/class	Pennant Nr.	Name	Crew/Troops	Displacement
Frigate (River)	F-101	ARD *Presidente Trujillo/Mella* (+)	107	2,125 tons
Frigate (River)	F-102	ARD *Juan Pablo Duarte*	107	2,360 tons
Frigate (Tacoma)	F-103	ARD *Presidente Troncoso/Gregorio Luperón* (+)	190	2,238 tons
Frigate (Tacoma)	F-104	ARD *Presidente Peynado/Cap.Gen. Pedro Santana* (+)	190	2,238 tons
Corvette (Flower)	C-101	ARD *Cristóbal Colón*	90	1,350 tons
Corvette (Flower)	C-102	ARD *Juan Alejandro Acosta*	90	1,350 tons
Corvette (Flower)	C-103	ARD *Juan Bautista Cambiaso*	90	1,350 tons
Corvette (Flower)	C-104	ARD *Gerardo Jansen*	90	1,350 tons
Corvette (Flower)	C-105	ARD *Juan Bautista Maggiolo*	90	1,350 tons
Destroyer (H)	D-101	ARD *Trujillo/Duarte* (+)	175	2,095 tons
Destroyer (F)	D-102	ARD *Generalísimo/Sánchez* (+)	145	2,095 tons
Minesweeper (Admirable)	BM-454	ARD *Separación*	104	650 tons
Minesweeper (Admirable)	BM-455	ARD *Tortuguero*	104	650 tons
LCI (L)	BDI-101	ARD *San Rafael*	24	285 tons
LCI (L)	BDI-102	ARD *17 de Julio*	24	285 tons
LCI (L)	BDI-103	ARD *Paraíso*	24	285 tons
LSM (LSM 1)	BA-104	ARD *Sirio*	58	1,095 tons
LSM (LSM 1)	BA-105	ARD *Anares*	58	1,095 tons
LCU (Samaná)	LA-1	ARD *Neyba*	15 + 36	310 tons
LCU (Samaná)	LA-2	ARD *Samaná*	15 + 36	310 tons
LCU (Samaná)	LA-3	ARD *17 de Julio*	15 + 36	310 tons
Patrol Boat (PC-173)	P-101	ARD *27 de Febrero*	65	463 tons
Patrol Boat (PC-173)	P-102	ARD *Capitán Wenceslao Arvelo*	65	463 tons
Patrol Boat (PC-173)	P-103	ARD *Constitución/Cibao*	65	463 tons
Patrol Boat (Argo)	P-104	ARD *Restauración*	44	370 tons
Patrol Boat (Argo)	P-105	ARD *Independencia*	44	370 tons
Patrol Boat (Argo)	P-106	ARD *Libertad*	44	370 tons
Patrol Boat (SC-110)	GC-101	ARD *Sánchez/30 de Marzo* (+)	27	85 tons
Patrol Boat (SC-110)	GC-102	ARD *Mella/Las Carreras* (+)	27	85 tons
Patrol Boat (SC-110)	GC-103	ARD *Rigel*	27	85 tons
Patrol Boat (SC-110)	GC-104	ARD	27	85 tons
Patrol Boat (AVR)	GC-105	ARD *Capitán Alsina*	35	100 tons
Patrol Boat (AVR)	GC-106	ARD *Capitán Maduro*	35	100 tons
Coast Guard boat (GC-1)	GC-1	ARD	12	37 tons
Coast Guard boat (GC-2)	GC-2	ARD	6	18 tons
Coast Guard boat (GC-1)	GC-3	ARD	12	37 tons
Coast Guard boat (GC-1)	GC-4	ARD	12	37 tons
Coast Guard boat (GC-1)	GC-5	ARD	12	37 tons
Coast Guard boat (GC-1)	GC-6	ARD	12	37 tons
Coast Guard boat (GC-1)	GC-7	ARD	12	37 tons
Coast Guard boat (GC-8)	GC-8	ARD	8	28 tons
Coast Guard boat (GC-9)	GC-9	ARD *Luperón/Las Calderas*	15	45 tons
Coast Guard boat (GC-9)	GC-10	ARD *22 de Julio/Bahía Ocoa*	15	45 tons
Coast Guard boat (GC-9)	GC-11	ARD *16 de Agosto/Bahía Manzanillo*	15	45 tons
Patrol Tug (-)	R-1	ARD *Macorix*	40	330 tons
Patrol Tug (-)	R-2	ARD *Caonabo*	40	330 tons
Speed Rescue Boat	LR-101	ARD	12	?
Speed Rescue Boat	LR-102	ARD	12	?
Speed Rescue Boat	LR-103	ARD	12	?
Presidential Yacht	-	ARD *Ramfis*	25	?
Steamer (-)	-	ARD *Presidente Trujillo* (*)	45	1,668 tons
Oil Tanker (294 Type)	BT-101	ARD *24 de Octubre*	25	?
Oil Tanker (294 Type)	BT-102	ARD *San Carlos*	25	?
Oil Tanker (-)	BT-4	ARD *Capitán W. Arvelo*	25	?
Floating dry dock	-	-	-	-
Floating crane	-	-	-	-

(*) Sunk by German Submarine U-156 on 21 May 1942 between Martinica and Puerto Rico.
(+) All these vessels were renamed after 1961.

Commanders of the Dominican Navy between 1949 and 1971: from left to right, Captain Manuel Perdomo, Vice Admirals Ramón Julio Didiez Burgos and César Augusto De Windt Lavandier; Brigadier General José García Trujillo, Vice Admiral Luis Homero Lajara Burgos, Admiral Rafael Richardson Lightbourne, Vice Admirals Tomás Emilio Cortiñas, Luis Ambrioso Facundo Esteva, Enrique Rafael Valdéz Vidaurre, Julio Alberto Rib Santamaría, Federico Betances Pierret and Ramón Emilio Jiménez Jr. (Armada de República Dominicana)

Table 10: Commanders of the Dominican War Navy 1949-1971[10]

Officer	Service dates
Captain Manuel Perdomo	16 April 1943 to 27 February 1947
Vice Admiral Julio Didiez Burgos	23 March 1947 to 16 April 1953
Vice Admiral César Augusto Windt Lavandier	16 April 1953 to 01 August 1953
Brigadier General (Army) José García Trujillo	01 August 1953 to 17 August 1953
Vice Admiral Luis Homero Lajara Burgos	17 August 1953 to 07 December 1954
Vice Admiral Rafael B. Richardson Lightbourne	01 February 1955 to 27 August 1956
Vice Admiral Tomás Emilio Cortiñas Criado	27 August 1956 to 23 March 1957
Vice Admiral Rafael B. Richardson Lightbourne	23 March 1957 to 19 September 1958
Vice Admiral Luis Ambrosio Facundo Esteva	19 September 1958 to 09 November 1961
Vice Admiral Enrique Rafael Valdéz Virraude	09 November 1961 to 21 January 1962
Vice Admiral Julio Alberto Rib Santamaría	21 January 1962 to 31 January 1964
Vice Admiral Federico Betances Pierret	31 January 1964 to 19 August 1964
Vice Admiral Ramón Emilio Jiménez Jr.	08 May 1965 to 02 July 1971

As for the Navy, its headquarters, based at Las Calderas Naval Base, was organised as follows:

- Chief of Staff and auxiliaries
- War Fleet
- Marine Infantry Corps
- Frogmen Commando Corps
- Naval Aviation Corps
- Department of Instruction and Personnel
- Department of Information and Communications
- Department of Naval Construction and Repairs
- Department of Artillery and Coastal Defence
- Department of Hydrography
- Department of Auxiliary Forces
- Directorate of Naval Health
- Merchant Marine
- Naval Reserve
- General Quartermaster
- Lighthouses and Buoys
- Music Band

Naval Aviation Corps (*Cuerpo de Aviación Naval*, CAN)

The Dominican Navy had a Naval Aviation Corps that existed for almost two years, between January 1951 to 3 November 1952. During that time, the AMD transferred a few aircraft to the Naval Aviation, the very first one being a Republic RC-3 Seabee amphibian, which received the serial GC-13 (for *Guardia Costera*, Coast Guard). Then the AMD also transferred four Catalinas, two PBY-5As and two OA-10As, which received the serials GC-14 to GC-17. The idea of the creation of a Naval Aviation was to assign the Navy the responsibility of patrolling the Dominican coasts, by sea and by air. President Trujillo, possibly influenced by his son Ramfis, reversed the decision after almost two years of air naval operations and all aircraft were returned to the AMD.

Marine Infantry Corps (*Cuerpo de Infantería de Marina*)

In December 1953, the Marine Corps was created, organised into a regiment with two battalions with a total of five companies. The command post of the regiment and its first battalion, with companies No. 1, 2, and 3, were at the *General Trujillo* Naval Base in Ciudad Trujillo (Santo Domingo, the capital), the second battalion with companies No.4 and No.5 at the *Jose Valdez Trujillo* Naval Base. Five years later it would be dissolved as Trujillo distrusted it, transferring the personnel to the Army and its amphibious vehicles to the Air Force.

In 1956, the Dominican Republic acquired a total of 25 Landsverk L-60L light tanks, 13 Landsverk Lynx armoured vehicles (also known as Pansarbil m/39), and 20 Bofors *Infanteriekannons* from Sweden. Surprisingly enough, these were not operated by the Dominican Army, but by the Armoured Battalion of the Dominican Military Aviation. The L-60Ls were armed with a 20mm Madsen cannon and a 7.62mm Madsen machine gun. Several were captured and operated by the rebels and three were destroyed during the fighting on 29 April 1965: one by an M40 recoilless rifle of the 82nd Airborne Division, US Army, another by an M50 Ontos and the third by a M48 Patton main battle tank of the 6th MEU, US Marine Corps. (Artwork by David Bocquelet)

In 1959, the Dominican Republic acquired a total of 15 AMX-13/75 light tanks from France. They were assigned to the Armoured Battalion of the AMD. Originally painted in dark blue overall, by 1961, when they were transferred to the CEFA, they had been repainted in olive green overall, as shown here. Several were secured by the rebels and at least one of them was destroyed by a M48 Patton main battle tank of the US Army. The survivors remained in service until the mid-1980s. (Artwork by David Bocquelet)

In 1959–1960, the Dominican Republic acquired two Sud Aviation SE.313E Alouette II and one Sud Aviation SE.319B Alouette III light helicopters from France. All three were painted in overall dark green (later on, in overall blue) and assigned to the *Aguilas* Rescue Squadron. As of 1965, they still represented the most modern helicopters of the AMD. However, all were withdrawn from service three years later. This is a reconstruction of the second of two Alouette IIs. (Artwork by Luca Canossa)

In exchange for granting basing rights to the US armed forces during the Second World War, starting in 1942 the Dominican Republic received limited quantities of Lend-Lease equipment, including the first North American T-6 Texan training aircraft. Over the following decade a large number of AT-6C/D, T-6D, Harvard, NA-44 and SNJ3/4s were acquired from different sources. Most were assigned to the Military Aviation School and served for training purposes, but this example is shown as wearing the insignia of the *Escuadrón de Caza* of the late 1950s. Dominican Texans were deployed for reconnaissance and as light ground-attack aircraft and saw active participation in counterinsurgency operations of the 1940s and into the early 1970s. Their principal armament consisted of three 7.62mm Browning machine guns and either unguided rockets or light bombs. This example is shown in markings introduced from 1949. (Artwork by Luca Canossa)

In 1946, the AMD purchased two Beech 18 light transports (serials 101 and 102), starting the service's long association with this type. By the mid-1950s, it additionally acquired seven UC-45F and C-45H Expeditors, as well as two AT-11 Kansan light bombers. While operated by the sole *Escuadrón de Transporte* (which also flew seven C-47Bs acquired starting from 1952), the two AT-11s were assigned to the *Escuadrón de Caza-Bombardeos*, armed with a pair of Browning machine guns installed in the nose and flown in counterinsurgency operations. This C-45 is shown as wearing markings introduced after 1949, including FAD roundels (applied in four positions) and a four-digit serial. (Artwork by Tom Cooper)

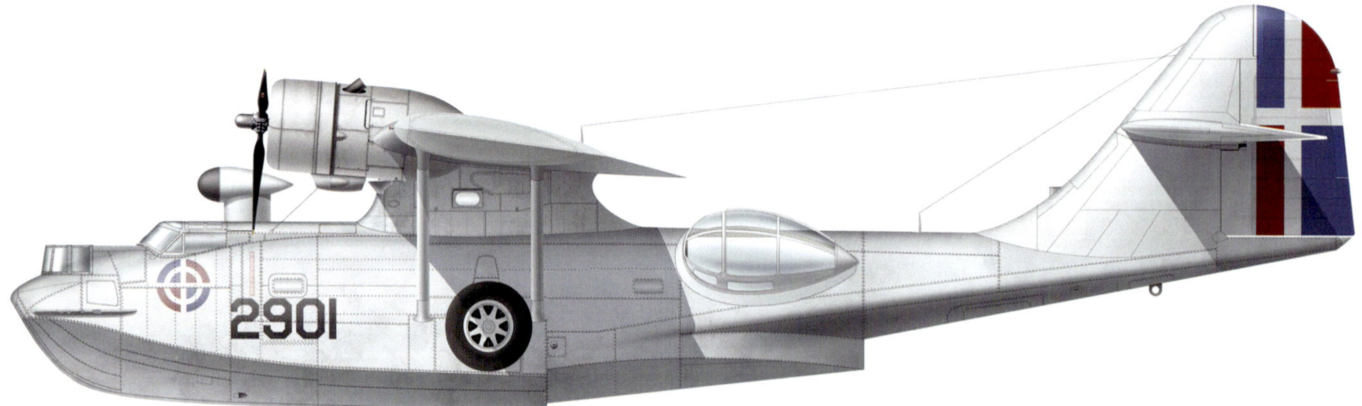

In 1946, the AMD purchased its first two Consolidated PBY-5A Catalina amphibians. By 1957, the Dominican Republic managed to acquire four additional PBY-6As and two OA-10As. Four were transferred to the Dominican Naval Aviation in 1951 but returned to the FAD a year later. Armed with three 12.7mm machine guns (two in the nose turret and one in the ventral hatch), and two 7.62mm machine guns (both in waist blisters), and painted in white overall, they were primarily deployed to patrol the coastline. In an emergency, they could be loaded with up to 4,000lbs of bombs or depth charges. (Artwork by Jean-Marie Guillou)

Following the failed invasion and coup attempt by a group of exiles in 1947, the Dominican Republic attempted to acquire large quantities of aircraft from the USA. Washington blocked all such attempts and similar negotiations with Canada. Nevertheless, by 1950, the AMD did manage to purchase a total of 11 Lockheed P-38 Lightning fighters from different sources, including four P-38Ls, two P-38Ms, and five F-5G (reconnaissance fighters). All arrived without any armament but received four 12.7mm Colt-Browning MG53-2 machine guns once they entered service. Painted in black overall, Dominican Lightnings received initial AMD roundels, applied in four positions. Before 1949, when four-digit serial numbering system was introduced, they received serials including two digits only. (Artwork by Jean-Marie Guillou)

In reaction to the events from 1947, in 1948, the AMD acquired two old B-17G Flying Fortress heavy bombers: one built by Vega and the other by Douglas. Both arrived in the Dominican Republic still in bare metal overall livery. They were later fully armed, including all their turrets, and Browning M2 machine guns in nine positions, as shown here. Each could load up to 8,000lbs (3,629kg) of bombs in their internal bomb bays. Eventually, both were painted in olive green on top surfaces and sides and remained in service until 1957. (Artwork by Jean-Marie Guillou)

In 1948, the Dominican Republic also obtained its first North American P-51 Mustangs. The first batch included one P-51A, one P-51C (shown here), two P-51D fighter-bombers, and a single F-6D reconnaissance aircraft. Except for a single P-51D painted in black, all were left in bare metal overall, but had their usual anti-glare panels in olive drab along the upper side of the forward fuselage. While still assigned to the *Compañía de Aviación* they wore AMD roundels and three-digit serials: four-digit serials were introduced in 1949. Acquired in disarmed condition, once in the Dominican Republic, the P-51A and P-51C each received just two 12.7mm Browning M2 machine guns, while the two P-51Ds were armed with their usual complement of six M2s. (Artwork by Jean-Marie Guillou)

Almost simultaneously with the acquisition of the first Mustangs, the AMD also purchased 10 radar-equipped Bristol Beaufighter TF.Mk 10 (Mk. VIF) night fighters thus becoming the only service in Central and Southern America to operate this type. All had a standardised camouflage pattern in medium sea grey (BS381C/637) and dark green (BS381C/641) on top surfaces and sides, and light aircraft grey (BS381C/627) on undersurfaces, and initially received three-digit serials and AMD roundels. Their armament included four internally installed 20mm Hispano Mk.II cannons, six 7.7mm Browning machine guns in the wings, one Browning for the gunner, and could additionally carry either eight RP-3 60lb unguided rockets or two 250lbs (125kg) bombs under their wings. In 1949, they received AMD markings and four-digit serials. (Artwork by Jean-Marie Guillou)

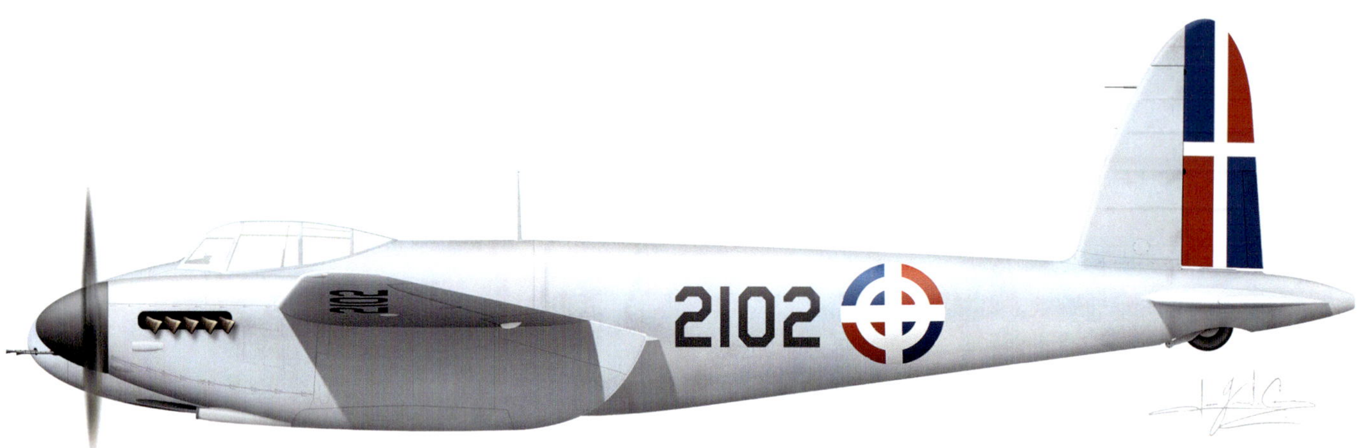

Along with the Beaufighters, in 1948, the AMD also purchased eight de Havilland Mosquito fighter-bombers, including five FB.Mk 6s and three T.Mk 29s armed conversion trainers. All were painted in high-speed silver overall. They initially received three-digit serials and AMD roundels; in 1949 these were changed to four-digit serials and AMD roundels. Their armament included four 20mm Hispano guns and four Browning M2s under the nose, and they could be armed with up to two 250lbs (125kg) bombs under the wing. While Beaufighters were withdrawn from service in 1956, Mosquitoes continued serving for two years longer. (Artwork by Luca Canossa)

Continuing its efforts to acquire additional US-made aircraft, in 1950, the AMD purchased five second-hand North American B-25 Mitchell light bombers, including one B-25C, one B-25G, one B-25H, and two B-25Js. All were equipped with 'solid' noses, containing four 12.7mm machine guns, and could carry up to 3,000lbs (1,360kg) of bombs in the internal bomb bay, but lacked the dorsal turret. Throughout their operational history with the AMD, which lasted until 1962, the Dominican Mitchells retained the bare metal overall livery. (Artwork by Jean-Marie Guillou)

After the government in Santo Domingo signed the Rio Treaty, the US gradually lifted its sanctions and the Dominican Republic was permitted to purchase 30 armed AT-6 trainers, the acquisition of which enabled the expansion of the *Compañía de Aviación* into an independent service, the *Fuerza Aérea Dominicana* (FAD) on 15 January 1948. Four years later, Washington then permitted the delivery of 25 Republic P-47D Thunderbolts from surplus stocks of the US Air Force to the AMD through the Reimbursable Aid Program (RAP). Thunderbolts arrived left in bare metal overall, with the usual anti-glare strip in olive drab applied along the upper side of the front and rear fuselage. They were fully armed with eight M2 machine guns, and could carry either up to 2,500lbs (1,250kg) of bombs, or up to 10 unguided rockets. (Artwork by Luca Canossa)

The new, powerful fighter-bombers entered service with the newly-established *Escuadrón de Caza Leónidas*. This was organised into five flights of four aircraft each: each flight was identified by a different colour applied on engine cowlings, wing-tips, underwing hardpoints, and tip of fins: yellow, orange, red, green, and blue. In addition to for four-digit serials applied in black on either side of the fuselage, underside of the left- and upper side of the right wing, they also wore one of the first five digits of the alphabet, denoting their position within the flight. (Artwork by Luca Canossa)

While failing in attempts to purchase US-made aircraft from Canada and Japan, in 1952 the government in Santo Domingo achieved a major breakthrough when reaching a deal with Sweden for delivery of 32 North American P-51D Mustang fighter-bombers. The aircraft arrived painted in bare metal overall, and wearing the usual anti-glare panel in olive drab along the upper front fuselage. They received four-digit serials and roundels in five positions, and then the gaudy markings of the *Escuadrón de Caza Ramfis* denoting them as operated by one of four flights (black, blue, red, and yellow), as well as individual numbers (applied in black on the fin) denoting the aircraft's position within the flight. (Artwork by Luca Canossa)

By 1961, all the 31 surviving P-51Ds lost their fancy insignia of the Trujillo-era and were repainted light grey overall (while retaining their anti-glare panels in olive drab). The unit operating them was also reorganised into the new *Escuadrón de Combate Dragones*. By 1965, the characteristic, big, four-digit, serials were moved to the fin and the Dominican flag on the rudder was overpainted in light grey. Mustangs saw heavy utilisation during the first weeks of the civil war, when they flew strikes on rebel positions in Santo Domingo. One was shot down by US Marines guarding the US Embassy. Surviving examples remained in service for 20 years longer. Dominican P-51Ds were fully armed, including six Browning M2s, and could carry either six or 10 unguided rockets, or a pair of 100-, 250-, or 500lbs bombs. (Artwork by Luca Canossa)

In 1955, the Dominican Republic landed another coup through the purchase of 25 de Havilland Vampire F.Mk 1s from Sweden. The aircraft initially retained the camouflage pattern applied in the country of origin, including olive green (FS24079) on top surfaces, and light blue gray (FS26176) on undersurfaces: initially, they were assigned to the *Escuadrón de Caza Ramfis*, but later transferred to the *Escuadrón de Caza Leonidas*. Their sole armament comprised four internally-installed Hispano Mk. 5 20mm guns. (Artwork by Luca Canossa)

Seventeen additional Vampire FB.Mk 50s were acquired from Sweden in 1967. By 1965, they were stripped of colours and repainted in high-speed silver finish overall. Operated by the *Escuadrón de Caza Leonidas*, they had their noses and fins painted in yellow or green. In addition to internally installed guns, FB.Mk 50s could also be armed with up to four RP-3 unguided 60lb rockets. They saw lots of action during the Dominican Civil War of 1965. Later during their careers, the surviving F.Mk 1s received a disruptive camouflage pattern consisting of tan colour partially over-sprayed atop of olive green. (Artwork by Luca Canossa)

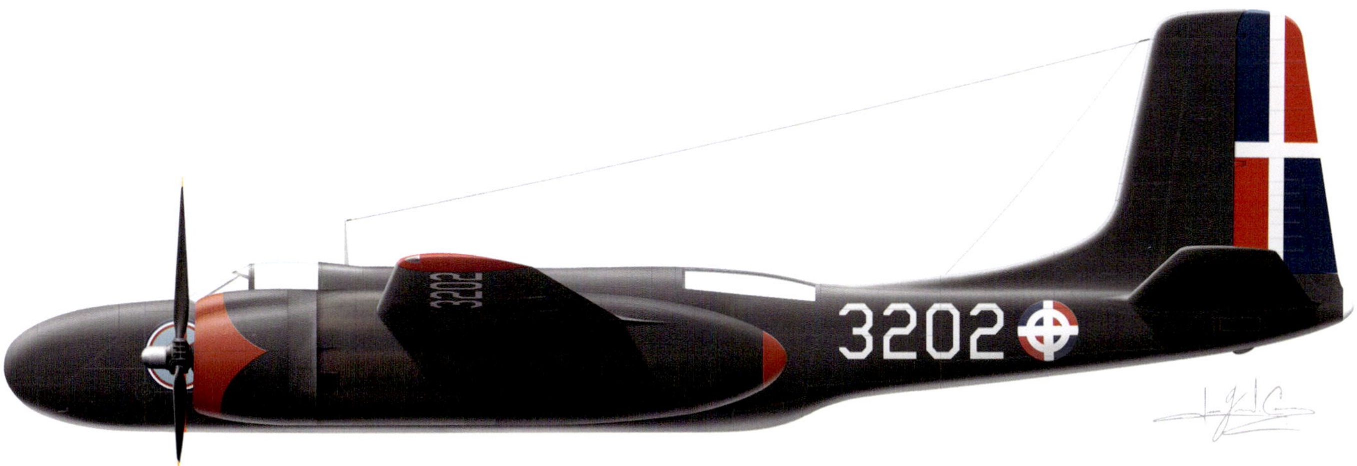

Aiming to replace worn-out B-25s, in 1959 the AMD acquired seven Douglas B-26 Invader light bombers. Painted in black overall, they were officially assigned to the Reconnaissance Squadron but wore the insignia of the *Escuadrón de Caza-Bombardeos*. While arriving without any armament, some of the Dominican Invaders were armed with up to four Browning M2 machine guns installed in the nose, and then with launch rails for unguided rockets, taken from Beaufighters. Additionally, they could carry up to 4,000lbs (2,000kg) of bombs in their bomb bay. The balance of the fleet was deployed for transport duties. Before being withdrawn from service, the survivors were stripped of colour and operated in bare metal overall, with engine cowlings in black. (Artwork by Luca Canossa)

In 1957, Santo Domingo was granted permission by the US to acquire four Lockheed AT-33 Shooting Star conversion trainers. Left in bare metal overall (though having their wing-tip tanks painted either in olive drab or black), they were armed with a pair of 12.7mm Browning machine guns and operated by the *Escuadrón de Caza Ramfis*. (Artwork by Tom Cooper)

In 1957–1958, the Dominican Republic acquired three helicopters of Sikorsky design, including two S-55Cs (1957) and one H-19 (1958). All were initially assigned to the Search and Rescue Flight of the *Ramfis* Squadron: later on, they were reassigned to the separate, *Aguilas* Search and Rescue Squadron. Initially painted in overall green, as shown here, they were later repainted in light grey overall. The last were withdrawn from service in 1969. (Artwork by Tom Cooper)

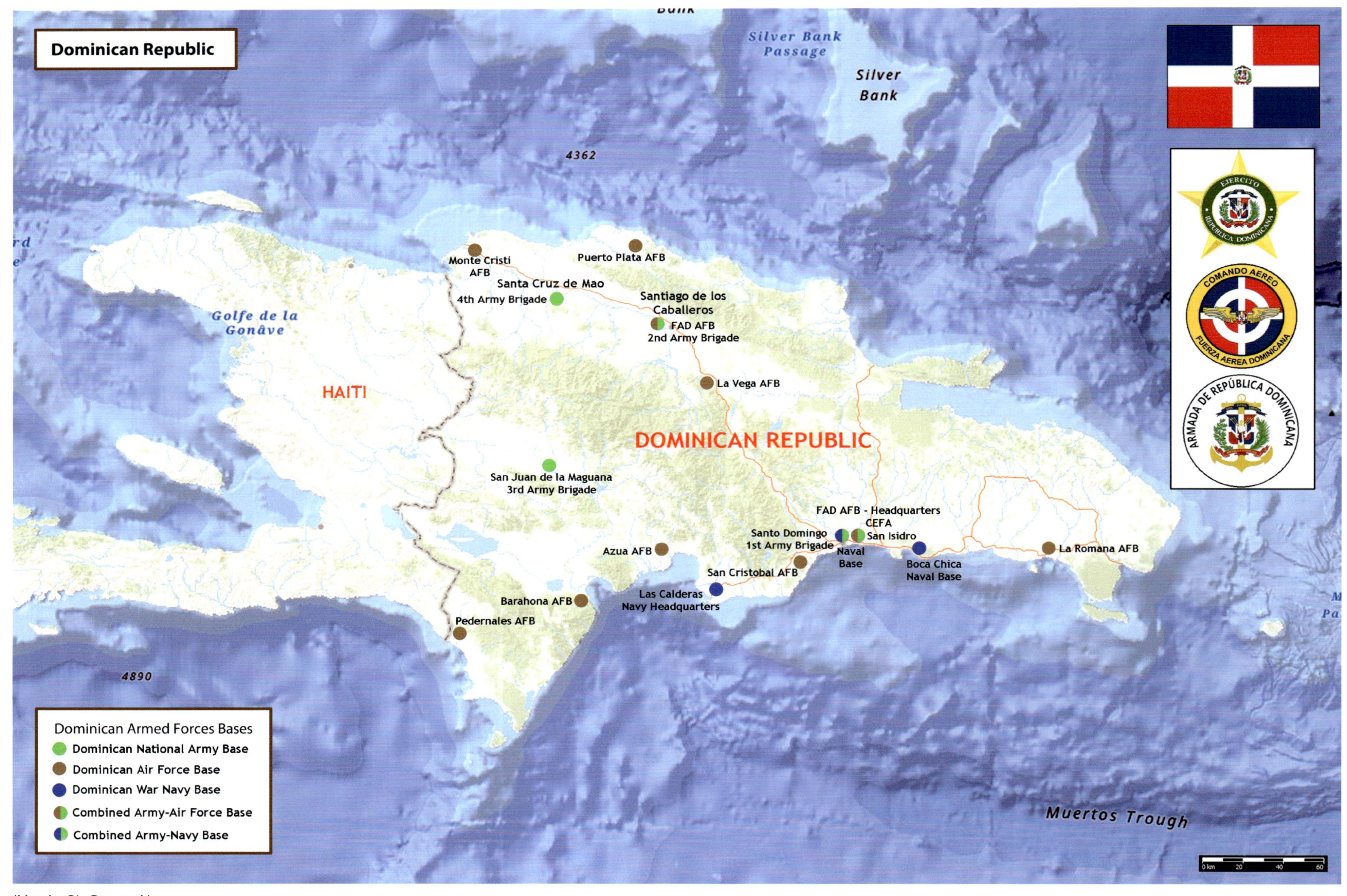

(Map by Pia Dworzak)

Three of the four PBY-5A Catalinas that, together with an RC-3 Seabee, were part of the small fleet of the Dominican Naval Aviation that barely lasted two years. (Armada de la República Dominicana)

Frogmen Commando Corps (*Cuerpo de Comandos de Hombres Ranas*)

In 1956, the Frogmen Corps was created, hiring Italian instructors who were Second World War veterans, including Colonel Illio Capocci, Captains Vitorio Tudesco, Alberto Cortelleza, Benito Pambianchi and Enzo Lobasto, plus civilians Elio Bolpi and Mamoru Matsunaga. The instructors at Calderas Naval Base at that time were the Ship Lieutenants Manuel Ramón Montes Arache, Francisco Alberto Caamaño Deñó, Julio A. Rib Santamaría and Jovanny Gutiérrez; in addition to eight Frigate Ensigns. The candidates for frogman training were Marine Corps officers. Up until the outbreak of the civil war in 1965, a total of 97 frogmen were trained. By then, Ship Captain Manuel Ramón Montes Arache became the Commander of the Frogmen Commando Corps, who fought on the Constitutionalist side in the April Revolution.

Ship Captain Manuel Ramón Montes Arache (left), commander of the Frogmen Corps, posing with Italian Colonel Illio Capocci, a Second World War veteran instructor (right). A group of frogmen posing with Captain Montes Arache (right). (*Armada de República Dominicana*)

Dominican National Police (*Policía Nacional Dominicana*, PND)

During the first US occupation of Santo Domingo from 1916 to 1924, American troops created a military institution called the *Guardia Nacional* (National Guard) in 1917, a military body that functioned as a defence and police agency, laying the foundations for the current National Police. Then on 2 July 1921 the Dominican National Police was created during the American occupation of the country. When the occupation forces left, the police corps was reorganised under the name of *Policía Municipal* (Municipal Police). In 1927, the name was again changed to *Brigada Nacional* (National Brigade).

The Dominican Congress issued Law 14 on 5 November 1930, which allowed the president of the Dominican Republic to appoint and dismiss local police chiefs. Finally, on 2 March 1936, the Dominican National Police (*Policía Nacional Dominicana*) was officially created through Decree No. 1523. From then on and until 1958, all the police chiefs were officers of the Dominican Army. On 9 June 1958, the first Police Chief that was trained in the institution was appointed, Colonel Ramón A. Soto Echavarría.

In 1959, the organic regulations of the police force were established and that year the General Inspectorate of Police was also created. In 1960, the Department of Traffic and Highways was created. In 1961, the Police Institution became dependent on the Ministry of the Interior, separating itself from the Army. That same year the Criminal Investigations Department was created. At that time the entire police force was made up of 2,716 personnel, including officers and NCOs. In 1962, the Cavalry Squadron was created within the police force, as well as the Armament Depot Administration and the Anti-Riot Department, a force known as the *Cascos Blancos* (White Helmets). Caamaño had been their commander. This force actively participated in the events of 1965. During Kennedy's administration, the *Cascos Blancos* were trained by two Spanish-speaking Los Angeles police officers in the tactics of riot control. This elite group of the Dominican Police was equipped by the United States with tear gas and batons.

On 15 April 1963, the Department of Transportation and Radio Patrol was created and a few months later the Engineering Department of the National Police.

On 13 January 1965, given the political upheaval that would later trigger the civil war, the Dominican National Police once again became dependent on the armed forces, increasing its strength to 8,300 effectives. That same year, the Information and Public Relations office of the National Police was created. After the Civil War, the White Helmets changed their name for *Cascos Negros* (Black Helmets).

Table 11: Dominican National Police Chiefs 1955-1967[11]

Officer	Service dates
Colonel Federico Fiallo	01 August 1955 to 10 September 1956
Colonel David Antonio Hart Dottin	10 September 1956 to 09 June 1958
Colonel Ramón A. Soto Echavarría	09 June 1958 to 09 March 1959
Major General Félix Hermida	09 March 1959 to 25 July 1959
Colonel David Antonio Hart Dottin	25 July 1959 to 11 February 1960
Colonel Braulio Sánchez	11 February 1960 to 01 January 1961
Colonel Luis Henriquez Montes de Oca	01 January 1961 to 21 July 1961
Colonel José Caonabo Fernández González	21 July 1961 to 06 September 1961
Colonel Marco Antonio Jorge Moreno	06 September 1961 to 28 November 1961
Colonel Rubén Antonio Tapia Cesse	28 November 1961 to 18 February 1962
Colonel Manuel Secundino Pérez Peña	18 February 1962 to 28 February 1962
Colonel Rafael de Castro Ortíz	28 February 1962 to 16 March 1962
Brigadier General Belisario Peguero	16 March 1962 to 18 January 1965
Colonel Hernán Despradel Brache	18 January 1965 to 10 February 1966
Brigadier General José de Jesús Morillo López	10 February 1966 to 01 August 1966
Brigadier General Luis Ney Tejada Álvarez	01 August 1966 to 28 March 1967

Officers of the Dominican National Police posing with their Indian motorcycles in the 1950s (left). Members of the Dominican National Police guarding the Government Palace in Santo Domingo during the civil war (right). (Policía Nacional Dominicana)

Chiefs of the Dominican National Police between 1955 and 1967: colonels Federico Fiallo, David Antonio Hart and Ramón Soto Echavarría, Major General Félix Hermida, Colonels Braulio Álvarez, Luis Enrique Montes de Oca, José Canoabo Fernández, Marco Antonio Moreno, Rubén Tapia Cesse, Manuel Pérez and Rafael de Castro Ortíz, Brigadier General Belisario Peguero, Colonel Hernán Despradel Brache, Brigadier Generals José de Jesús Morillo and Luis Ney Tejada. (Policía Nacional Dominicana)

3

CRISIS IN THE ARMED FORCES: LOYALISTS VERSUS CONSTITUTIONALISTS

Introduction

After the assassination of the dictator Generalissimo Rafael Leónidas Trujillo in 1961 and the subsequent governments, including that of Juan Bosch, who had won the first truly democratic elections in the Dominican Republic in 1962 and who wanted to impose a series of reforms that would affect the more conservative sectors that in one way or another were linked to Trujillo, a crisis began to arise. That crisis started within the Dominican political class and especially in the armed forces, with two well-differentiated antagonistic groups emerging: those loyal to the *Trujillista* principles, who wanted to maintain their privileges at all costs, and those who adhered to the Constitution and supported former President Bosch, who had been overthrown by a military coup in September 1963. He was the victim of a dirty campaign by the Catholic Church and conservative sectors that accused him of being a communist.

Professor Bosch won the elections with around 58.72 percent of the votes, so it was a legitimate regime, but he proposed a democratic program in the state protected by the 1963 Constitution, and in the government program of the PRD itself, and that was unacceptable for the power players of that time. Bosch immediately carried out a profound restructuring of the country. On 29 April 1963, a new liberal constitution was promulgated that granted rights unknown to Dominicans. Among other things, it established labour rights and freedom of association, and addressed traditionally excluded sectors such as pregnant women, illegitimate children, homeless people, children, the family, youth and farmers, among others. Bosch faced traditionally powerful sectors. His attitude against the large estates brought him the animosity of the landowner sector. The Catholic Church believed that Bosch was trying to secularise the country. The industrialists were suspicious of the benefits that the

President Juan Bosch with FAD Commander Brigadier General Miguel Atila Luna inspecting a P-51D Mustang fighter in 1963 (left). President Bosch with Colonel Caamaño greeting people (right). (Albert Grandolini Archives)

The three legalist and anti-communist generals of the Dominican Armed Forces: from left to right, Major General Víctor Elby Viñas Román, Brigadier Generals Elías Wessin y Wessin and Antonio Imbert Barreras. They had planned the coup d'état that overthrew President Bosch in 1963. (Open Source)

new Constitution granted to the working class. The military, who previously enjoyed the freedom to do whatever they wanted, felt that Bosch was subjugating them.

The 1963 coup d'état in the Dominican Republic took place on 25 September of that year against President Juan Bosch, who only had seven months in power. At the beginning of the uprising against Bosch, Coronel Wessin y Wessin (he was promoted to General in 1964) controlled the Armed Forces Training Centre (CEFA), an elite group of about 2,000 highly trained infantry personnel. This quasi-independent organisation, originally established by Ramfis Trujillo, son of the former dictator, was formed to protect the government. Stationed at San Isidro Air Base, they differed from regular Army units by being equipped with tanks, recoilless rifles and artillery, as well as their own attack aircraft. General Elías Wessin declared: 'The communist, Marxist-Leninist, Castroist doctrine, or whatever it is called, is now outlawed'.[1]

The military coup was led by the then Secretary of the Armed Forces, Major General Víctor Elby Viñas Román, with the support of Colonel Elías Wessin y Wessin and other military leaders. Through a manifesto, they dissolved the legislative chambers, suppressed the Constitution of April of that year as well as all the acts issued under that Substantive Charter. A Provisional Military Junta assumed control of the government until a government made up of civilians would be formed.

Bosch went into exile in Puerto Rico. The United States condemned the coup d'état, suspending aid to the country and refusing to recognise the military junta.

Causes of the Revolution

The country's debt was $11 million and when the triumvirate fell it was at $150 million, mainly due to corruption. This triumvirate was only able to remain in power thanks to the support of the United States, the Catholic Church and the pro-Trujillo generals to whom it gave different extraordinary privileges such as opening canteens to sell contraband products brought in on Air Force planes. The officers involved included Belisario Peguero, Apolinar Alfredo Montás Guerrero, Gaspar Salvador Morató Pimentel, Rubén Darío González Nuñez, Hernán Despradel Brache, José de Jesús Morillo López and Dr. Antonio de los Santos Almarante. All of were active high-ranking officers of the National Police. The list was headed by the head of the National Police himself, General Belisario Peguero.

The situation that prevailed after the resurgence of the roots of Trujillo's Dominican Party caused Dr. Joaquín Balaguer, who had founded the Dominican Social Reformist Party (*Partido Reformista Social Dominicano*, PRSC) in New York, and Professor Juan Bosch to join in an agreement signed in Río Piedras, Puerto Rico, in which they agreed to join forces to overthrow the triumvirate. Their joint action would undermine the triumvirate through constant strikes by workers in state companies and public transport drivers. This forced the triumvirate to keep the police on the streets to quell the riots and arrest union, political and student leaders.

The populist alliance of Bosch and Balaguer had the support of right-wing businessmen and landowners who created a new party called the Evolutionary Liberal Party (*Partido Liberal Evolucionista*), headed by Luís Amiama Tió (one of the two survivors of those who executed Trujillo).

Reid Cabral, seeking to appease the people, opened the elections for September 1965 but without the participation of Professor Bosch and Dr. Balaguer, leaders of the two major parties.

Bosch continued to organise conspiracies against the triumvirate from Puerto Rico with the support of unions and student groups, to which was added the group of soldiers who were dissatisfied with the poor treatment of their superiors, who were benefited by the triumvirate. This was the base of the Constitutionalists, who were created by Lieutenant Colonel Fernández Domínguez as a result of the coup d'état, and gained strength after many soldiers who supported the coup realised how corrupt the military leaders were, that was the true origin of the Constitutionalists who sought to go back to the democratic path established by the 1963 elections. The so-called Loyalists were from the conservative sectors, and of course the *Trujillista* militaries.[2]

The two antagonistic groups, however, had a common objective, to get rid of President Reid Cabral, in the case of the Constitutionalists, to enable the return of Bosch and in the case of the Legalists, to establish a new military junta.

Leales versus *Constitucionalistas*

Between 1963 and 1965, two antagonistic groups formed and finally ended up facing each other in a terrible and bloody civil war:

Leales (Loyalists): This group was composed of: Training Centre of the Dominican Armed Forces (CEFA), much of the Army, the entire Air Force and although the Navy was supposedly

President Donald Reid Cabral at a press conference at the beginning of the civil war in April 1965 (left). President Reid with the US *charge d'affairs* William Connett and US naval attaché Ralph Heywood in an emergency meeting at the beginning of the civil war (right). (Centro León collection)

neutral at first, it later became part of this group. This sector was later supported by American military forces through the United States Marine Corps (USMC) and the 82nd Airborne Division of the US Army, plus the Inter-American Peace Force (IAPF) with Brazilian, Paraguayan, Honduran, Nicaraguan Army troops and a Costa Rican police force. Besides those countries mentioned, the Loyalists had also the international support of France, Spain, Federal Republic of Germany, The Netherlands, United Kingdom, Peru, Mexico, El Salvador, Pakistan, Israel, South Africa, Argentina and India. During the civil war, the Loyalist military commanders were generals Elías Wessin y Wessin and Antonio Imbert Barrera, and Colonel Pedro Bartolomé Benoit. They led approximately 1,800 troops.

Constitucionalistas (Constitutionalists): This group consisted mainly of officers, NCOs and troops who supported former President Juan Bosch, members of the PRD, the PRSC and the Dominican Communist Party (*Partido Comunista Dominicano*). Internationally, this group was supported by Costa Rica, Sri Lanka, People's Republic of China, Cuba, Yugoslavia and Sweden. During the civil war, the Constitutionalist were led by colonels Francisco Caamaño Deñó, Manuel Montes Arache and Fernández Domínguez. They had approximately 1,300 troops.

Donald Reid Cabral, who became head of the junta on 23 December 1963, was unpopular with most high-ranking officers in the Army for his attempt to cut their privileges. Reid suspected that some or all of these officers would try to overthrow him in the spring of 1965. Hoping to prevent a coup d'état, on 24 April 1965, he sent his chief of staff, General Marcos Rivera, to detain four officers considered conspirators. They did not surrender, but rather took a military camp northwest of Santo Domingo and captured Rivera. Later, taking advantage of the uprising, the Dominican Revolutionary Party and the 14 June Revolutionary Movement put a large number of armed civilians on the streets, giving rise to the creation of the first armed squads of the rebels, who were known generally as 'Commandos'.[3] These were, at times, well-armed gangs of teenagers. The Dominican Popular Movement distributed Molotov cocktails to the crowds and the rebel military established defensive positions on the Duarte Bridge to prevent the CEFA military from crossing it and entering Santo Domingo. The Dominican Civil War had just started.

The pro-Bosch rebels, known as *Constitutionalists* for advocating the restoration of President Bosch and the restoration of the 1963 Constitution, took to the streets. The commander of the National Guard, who was not part of the rebels, had negotiated with Colonel Hernando Ramírez, leader of the rebels, and took Reid Cabral and his other cabinet member prisoners, and handed over the National Palace to the rebels. The rebels also seized government media outlets in the capital.

Fendandez Domínguez created the *Enriquillo* Movement based around soldiers who wanted to see the country with a democratic system after the 1963 coup and this evolved into the Constitutionalist movement. The *Plan Enriquillo* was based on several premises:

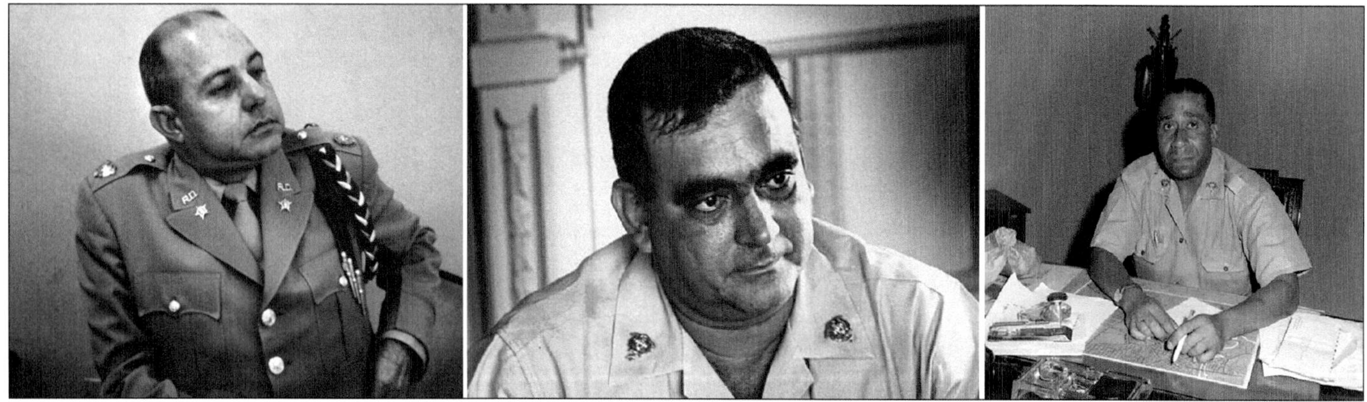

Some Loyalist military leaders: From left to right, Generals Antonio Imbert Barrera and Elías Wessin y Wessin, and Colonel Pedro Bartolomé Benoit. (Open source)

Some Constitutionalist military leaders: from left to right, Colonel Francisco Caamaño Deñó, Navy Captain Manuel Montes Arache and Colonel Rafael Fernández Domínguez. (Open source)

surprise and speed, the opportunism of the military leaders who did not belong to the movement, and the antipathy that many of them felt for General Wessin.

Both Colonel Francisco Alberto Caamaño and Navy Captain Manuel Ramón Montes Arache joined the rebels on the night of 26 April. Colonel Hernando Ramírez was in charge of the revolt until 27 April, when he handed over command to Caamaño. Colonel Rafael Tomás Fernández Domínguez was not in the country; he was in Chile as a military attaché, and he found out about the revolt there in Chile.

José Rafael Molina Ureña, who was the head of the Chamber of Deputies during the Bosch government, became Provisional President until Bosch could return. In the days that followed, the Constitutionalists clashed with internal security agents and the right-wing CEFA military. By 26 April 1965, armed civilians outnumbered the regular rebel military. *Radio Santo Domingo*, now under full control of the rebels, began inciting violent actions.

Both sides were heavily armed and many civilians were caught in the crossfire. The US government began preparations for the evacuation of its citizens and other foreigners who may wish to leave the Dominican Republic. The degree of participation of communists, including the 14 June Revolutionary Movement, had been questioned.

The Constitutionalist Provisional President Molina Ureña and Colonel Hernando Ramírez asked the United States Ambassador for American mediation to stop attacks by the Dominican Air Force on the Constitutionalist areas. The US Ambassador refused. Totally dismayed by this rejection, Molina Ureña resigned. At San Isidro Air Base, the heads of CEFA, the Navy and the FAD created a military junta following instructions from the American military attachés. They had tried to negotiate the creation of a military junta with the rebels to avoid a civil war, but it was not possible as Colonel Ramírez followed the instructions of Lieutenant Colonel Fernández Dominiguiez to return to democracy. The senior military officers were convinced that if Bosch was going to become president, they would put him in prison and that is why they decided to follow the Americans' plan. The head of the military junta was Colonel Pedro Bartolomé Benoit.

On 27 April, the Dominican Air Force resumed its attack against Constitutionalist positions in Santo Domingo using its F-51D and Vampire fighters which strafed and fired rockets while armed rebel civilians invaded a police station and summarily executed the police officers. On the following day, the rebels stormed the Ozama Fortress. An AMX-13 tank was used, which with one shot made a hole in the fortress wall, and then the tank penetrated into the fortress's courtyard followed by the rebel troops made up of armed military and civilians, and released 700 prisoners from the that fortress's prison. There was also a warehouse of infantry weapons, mortars and anti-tank weapons in the fortress; most of the weapons were distributed to civilians, and the creation of 'commandos' began, which were organised by communist militants trained in Cuba and Eastern Europe.

The swearing in ceremony of Provisional President José Rafael Molina Ureña. (Public Domain)

4

OPERATION POWER PACK. THE US INTERVENTION IN THE DOMINICAN REPUBLIC IN 1965–1966

Background

President Lyndon Johnson's 30 April 1965 decision to intervene in the Dominican Civil War reflected pervasive concerns about a communist takeover similar to that which occurred after the Cuban Revolution in 1959. His decision also occurred amidst the escalating American military intervention in Vietnam. By April 1965 two powerful factions had emerged, the Loyalists and the Constitutionalists. The Loyalists, who wanted to install a military junta and the Constitutionalists, supported by elements of the military, backed the exiled socialist politician Juan Bosch, who had briefly held the Dominican Republic's presidency in 1963 before being ousted in a coup, and wanted his liberalising constitution reinstated. The fact was that both sides were tired of President Reid, which was the only thing in common between them. On 24 April 1965 President Reid was arrested and the two rival groups decided to form their own governments, and thus civil war broke out.

Occupation

The United States planned the intervention within 24 hours of the outbreak of civil war, since military advisors were looking for a way to stop the rebels, and they urged the head of the Navy and the FAD to form a military junta supported by the USA.

The decision to intervene militarily in the Dominican Republic was made by United States President Lyndon Johnson. Convinced of the defeat of the Loyalist forces and fearing the emergence of 'a second Cuba' in the Caribbean, he ordered the US armed forces to restore order. The United States neglected to consult with OAS members before acting, using as an excuse that they had to act quickly.

Until then, all civilian advisors had been against immediate intervention, hoping that the Loyalist side could end the civil war. President Johnson, however, followed the advice of his ambassador in Santo Domingo, William Tapley Bennett, who questioned the inefficiency and indecision of the Dominican military leaders. Bennett suggested that the US interpose its forces between the rebels and the junta, thereby enforcing a ceasefire. The United States then asked the OAS to negotiate a political agreement between the opposing factions.

Chief of Staff General Earle Gilmore Wheeler told Lieutenant General Bruce Palmer of the US XVIII Airborne Corps: 'Its occupation without prior notice is to prevent the Dominican Republic from becoming communist'.[1]

On 29 April, under the official argument of the need to protect the lives of foreigners, none of whom had been killed or wounded, a fleet of six US Navy ships was sent to blockade the island and thus the invasion by ground troops began, including the Marine Corps and part of the 82nd Airborne Division. Also, around 75 members of Company "E" of the 7th Special Forces Group (Green Berets) were deployed. Ultimately, a contingent of 30,000 soldiers and marines was sent to Santo Domingo. The naval units of the Caribbean Ready Group, also known as Task Group TG-44.9, were formed

United States President Lyndon Baines Johnson (1963–1969). (Public Domain). On the right, President Johnson huddles with advisors in the Cabinet Room of the White House on 28 April 1965, just before delivering his televised speech announcing the deployment of US Marines into Santo Domingo in the Dominican Republic. From left to right: George Ball, Dean Rusk, President Johnson, Jack Valenti, Richard Goodwin, unidentified, George Reedy, McGeorge Bundy, unidentified. (Yoichi Okamoto/LJB Library)

From left to right: William Tapley Bennett Jr, US Ambassador to the Dominican Republic; Lieutenant General Earle Gilmore Wheeler, US Army Chief of Staff and Lieutenant General Bruce Palmer, XVIII Airborne Corps. (Public Domain)

into Amphibious Squadron Ten, consisting of the helicopter carrier LPH-4 USS *Boxer*, high-speed transport APD-89 USS *Ruchamkin*, attack cargo ship AKA-103 USS *Rankin*, amphibious transport dock LPD-1 USS *Raleigh*, landing ship dock LSD-30 USS *Fort Snellings*, the landing ship tank LST-1178 USS *Wood County* and some other minor vessels. Its Commander was Commodore James A. Dare.

President Lyndon B. Johnson declared that night that he had given orders for the landing of marines in Santo Domingo in order to protect the lives of American citizens and that the OAS had been informed of this situation. Other versions claim the invasion was carried out unilaterally and that the OAS delegates found out about the invasion on radio and television after Johnson's speech. However, shortly after, the United States, together with the OAS, formed the Inter-American Peace Force for intervention in the Dominican Republic, whose actions are described in the second volume.

The revolution took on the dimension of a civil war, when the CEFA Forces, led by General Elías Wessin y Wessin, plus the Army's *Enriquillo* Battalion from San Cristóbal struck back against the Constitutionalists on 25 April. Despite tank attacks and aerial bombardments by Loyalist forces, the Constitutionalists still maintained their positions in the capital and attempted to extend the conflict to secure control of the entire country. The Venezuelan economist José Antonio Mayobre, representing the Secretary General of the United Nations, acted unsuccessfully as a mediator between the parties in conflict during the crisis in the Dominican Republic.

Evacuation of US and Foreign Nationals

In response to the rapidly deteriorating situation on 25 April President Johnson directed the Joint Chiefs of Staff (JCS) to prepare to evacuate American nationals. Two days later, unarmed

Helicopter carrier LPH-4 USS *Boxer* with 16 USMC Sikorsky UH-34 Sea Horse helicopters on deck, plus one flying nearby. (US Navy)

High-speed transport APD-89 USS *Ruchamkin*. (US Navy)

Attack cargo ship AKA-103 USS *Rankin*. (US Navy)

Amphibious transport dock LPD-1 USS *Raleigh*. (US Navy)

LSD-30 USS *Fort Snellings* (left) and LST-1178 USS *Wood County* (right). (US Navy)

Clockwise: US Marines landing on Dominican soil in April 1965. A USMC UH-34A taking off from USS *Boxer* carrying supplies for the marines while in the back a CH-37 Mojave waits for its turn. Some troops were helicoptered to Haina on board UH-34s and went directly to the El Embajador Hotel in Santo Domingo. (USMC Archives via Albert Grandolini)

American citizens being gathered at El Embajador Hotel to be evacuated by the marines and then some were airlifted by UH-34A helicopters to the US Navy ships. (USMC Archives via Albert Grandolini)

Most US citizens and other foreign nationalities were taken to the Port of Haina and directly boarded US Navy ships to be taken to Puerto Rico. (Albert Grandolini Archives)

The first two places where the marines established defensive perimeters; the El Embajador Hotel (left) and the American Embassy in Santo Domingo (right). (Open source)

marines from USS *Boxer* helicoptered to Haina (10 miles south-west of Santo Domingo) to evacuate American civilians brought from the Hotel El Embajador in Santo Domingo. The next day a platoon of marines landed at Haina, proceeded to the hotel and established a helipad on the nearby polo field from which nearly 700 civilians were evacuated between that and the following day.

American Stability Operations

Unfortunately, the situation in Santo Domingo continued to deteriorate. On 28 April harassment of Americans continued, there was fire near the US Embassy and Ambassador William Bennett reported 'collective madness' engulfing the city. After receiving an early morning written request on 29 April for help from the Loyalists, at 7:30 pm, President Johnson authorised the use of overwhelming force to stabilise the situation. Soldiers from the 82nd Airborne Division and marines from the 4th Marine Expeditionary Brigade were dispatched to reinforce the American Embassy, protect American nationals in Santo Domingo, and prevent a communist takeover. The president recognised that by bypassing the OAS, American unilateral action would cause diplomatic tensions with OAS members, but he remained confident enough members could be convinced to offer support after the situation improved.

The stability operations, which lasted from 30 April to 3 May, can be separated into three phases:

- The landing at San Isidro Airfield (about 10 miles east of Santo Domingo);
- The eight-mile advance west from the airfield to the Ozama River;
- The establishment of a line of communications to link the airfield with the International Security Zone (ISZ) around the US Embassy, thereby separating the two factions.

The operation was based on JCS Operation Plan 310/2, which had been rehearsed several times, but did not include current political or geographic information.

The 4th Marine Expeditionary Brigade (4th MEB), whose Commanding Officer was Major General John G. Bouker, deployed in the Dominican Republic was organised as shown in Table 12.[2]

The 6th MEU had 131 officers and 1,571 marines and they were equipped with M14 and M16 rifles, UH-34 helicopters, M48A3 Patton tanks, M50 Ontos, LVTP-5s and artillery.

Table 12: 4th Marine Expeditionary Brigade Organisation

Unit	**Commanding Officer**
6th Marine Expeditionary Unit (MEU)	Colonel George W. Daughtry
Battalion Landing Team 1/6	Lieutenant Colonel William F. Doehler
Headquarters and Service Company	Captain John G. Flynn
Company A	Captain Merle G. Sorenson
Company B	Captain Richard L. Evans
Company C	Captain Donald F. Tremmel
Company D	Captain John J. Rozman
Battalion Landing Team 3/6	Lieutenant Colonel Paul F. Pedersen
Headquarters and Service Company	Captain Donald Festa
Company I	Captain William G. Davies
Company K	Captain Robert C. Cockell
Company L	Captain Horace W. Baker
Company M (Gitmo, based in Guantánamo, Cuba)	Captain Paul A. Wilson, Jr.
Battalion Landing Team 1/8	Lieutenant Colonel Edward F. Danowitz
Headquarters and Service Company	Captain Russell I. Hudson
Company A	Captain Joseph Loughran
Company B	1st Lieutenant Donald B. Evans
Company C	Captain Paul K. Dougherty
Company D	Captain Charles Barstow
Battalion Landing Team 1/2 (Reserve)	Lieutenant Colonel James E. Harrell
Headquarters and Service Company	1st Lieutenant William J. Hayes III
Company A	Captain Robert C. Knowles
Company B	Captain Arthur P. Brill, Jr.
Company C	Captain Edmund Keefe, Jr
Company D	1st Lieutenant Robert J. O'Brien
2nd Battalion, 10th Marines	Major Kenneth C. Williams
Headquarters Battery	1st Lieutenant Joseph M. Warren
Howtar Battery 2/10	1st Lieutenant George W. Thurmond (1–20 May) 1st Lieutenant Herbert W. Degraff (20–29 May)
Howtar Battery 3/10	1st Lieutenant Sidney B. Grimes (29 April–26 May) 1st Lieutenant Thomas E. Mossy (26 May–6 June)
Battery E	Captain Joseph C. Mayers
Battery F	Captain William D. Benjamin
Prov MAG-60	Lieutenant Colonel James E. Fegley
VMF (AW)-451 *Warlords* Squadron (F-8 Crusader fighters)	Lieutenant Colonel Dellwyn L. Davies
VMFA-323 *Death Rattlers* Squadron (F-4 Phantom fighters)	Lieutenant Colonel Norman W. Gourley
HMM-263 *Thunder Chickens* Squadron (UH-34 helicopters)	Lieutenant Colonel Truman Clark
HMM-264 *Black Knights* Squadron (HUS-1 helicopters)	Lieutenant Colonel Frederick M. Kleppsattel, Jr.
Logistical Support Group	Major Joseph F. Schoen, Jr.

The first contingents of Marines boarding UH-34A Sea Horse helicopters bound for Santo Domingo. (USMC Archives)

The huge Marine camp near El Embajador Hotel in Santo Domingo (left). Marines disembarking from the UH-34s near the aforementioned hotel (right). (USMC Archives)

USMC Vought F-8 Crusader fighters of VMF (AW)-451 *Warlords* Squadron being refuelled in flight during the deployment to Puerto Rico (left). Pilots of Marine Squadron VMF (AW)-451 posing next to an F-8 fighter in Puerto Rico during the Dominican Crisis (right). (USMC Archives)

Another USMC air squadron deployed to Puerto Rico during the Dominican Civil War was VMFA-323 *Death Rattlers* with their F-4 Phantom fighters. (USMC Archives)

USMC M48A3 Patton tanks at the Camp in Santo Domingo (top left). A Marine LVTP-5 vehicle and an M50 Ontos (bottom left). A column of USMC M50 Ontos and a LVTP-5 moving through the streets of Santo Domingo. (USMC Archives)

The US Army 82nd Airborne Division, spearheaded by the 3rd Brigade, had Major General Robert H. York as its commanding officer. Its components were as shown in Table 13. Most US Army troopers were armed with the then-new M16 assault rifle.

Table 13: Organisation of 3rd Brigade, US 82nd Airborne Division

3rd Brigade
1st Battalion (Airborne), 505th Infantry
2nd Battalion (Airborne), 505th Infantry
1st Battalion (Airborne), 508th Infantry
Artillery
2nd Battalion (Airborne), 321st Artillery (105mm)
Brigade Aviation
Company A, 82nd Aviation Battalion, with 8 Bell UH-1B and 16 UH-1D helicopters, plus a few Bell OH-13Hs
Brigade Reconnaissance
Troop B, 1st Squadron (Armored), 17th Cavalry
Company O (Ranger), 75th Infantry
Brigade Support
82nd Support Battalion
58th Signal Company
Company C, 307th Engineer Battalion (Airborne)
408th Army Security Agency Detachment
518th Military Intelligence Detachment
307th Medical (Airborne) Headquarters and Alpha Company

Phase 1: Landing

On 26 April US Continental Army Command notified XVIII Airborne Corps to place the 82nd Airborne Division, commanded by Major General Robert York, on Defense Condition 3 (DEFCON 3) at Fort Bragg, NC.[3] At 4:30 pm, 29 April, the JCS designated General York commander of US Ground Forces, Dominican Republic, and shortly thereafter Atlantic Command directed him initiate Operation Power Pack I.

US Army 82nd Airborne Division paratroopers getting ready to board a fleet of C-130E Hercules aircraft to be deployed to the Dominican Republic in April 1965. (US Army Archives)

A USAF C-124C Globemaster II and several C-130Es taxiing at the FAD San Isidro Air Base in April 1965. (USAF Archives)

A USAF C-130E Hercules on the ramp at San Isidro AFB. In the back, an impressive flight line of FAD P-51D Mustang fighters (left). A giant Douglas C-124C Globemaster II on the ramp at San Isidro AFB. Some US paratroopers waiting to be deployed to Santo Domingo (right). (USAF via Albert Grandolini)

At the time of the alert, 70 C-130s were available at Pope AFB, NC, but there were also 46 from the Military Air Transport Service (MATS) and 39 from Tactical Air Command (TAC) bases to be ready at DEFCON 2. Besides, six MATS C-124 Globemaster II aircraft were also available to transport bulky equipment not suitable for C-130s. Originally, two airborne battalion combat teams from the 3rd Brigade, 82nd Airborne Division were to layover in Puerto Rico before parachuting near San Isidro Airfield, eight miles east of Santo Domingo. However, concerned that the Loyalists could not hold out until morning, Secretary of Defense Robert McNamara and General Earle Wheeler, Chairman of the JCS, ordered the brigade to land directly by airplane at San Isidro AFB, rather than parachuting. They also worried parachuting would appear too aggressive. Although landing at San Isidro airport resulted in congestion, it proved fortunate because sharp coral outcroppings covered the nearby parachute drop zone.

At 9:30 pm, Vice Admiral Kleber Masterson, aboard USS *Boxer*, received news of the 82nd Airborne Division's imminent arrival and dispatched his aide and two Marine captains to the airfield. They convinced the Loyalist forces to open the control tower, turn on the runway lights, and talk down the airplanes.

Meanwhile, on the morning of 29 April, right after the US troops and equipment were loaded on the planes, a Boeing EC-135 airborne command post with a command group aboard flew to Ramey AFB in Puerto Rico together with a C-130 with communication gear and operators. Originally, the fleet of USAF C-130s were going to land at Ramey AFB but it was ordered to have them land directly at San Isidro AFB in the Dominican Republic. The EC-135 took off from Ramey AFB and the personnel on board diverted the incoming C-130 traffic to San Isidro.

US Navy Vice Admiral Kleber Masterson. (US Navy Archives)

A US Army Bell UH-1D from Company A, 82nd Aviation Battalion in Santo Domingo (left). Several US Army Bell OH-13Hs were also deployed in the Dominican Republic (right). (US Army Archives)

A USAF Boeing EC-135 was used to guide the C-130 fleet with paratroopers to San Isidro AFB (top). USAF Ramey AFB in Puerto Rico (bottom). (USAF Archives)

Captain John F. Burnside, executive officer of the 82nd Aviation Battalion on his chopper (left). US Army Bell UH-1B helicopters at San Isidro AFB (right). (US Army Archives via Albert Grandolini)

The first plane, carrying General York, touched down at 02:16 am, on 30 April and within four hours 33 C-130s delivered the two battalion combat teams, with another 40 C-130s and six C-124s with equipment, vehicles, tanks, pieces of artillery, ammunition, etc. Sixty-five other C-130s had to land at Ramey AFB since the facilities in San Isidro AFB were saturated. Once the troops were disembarked in San Isidro, the empty C-130s flew to Ramey and more troops were sent to the Dominican Republic.

Lieutenant General Bruce Palmer, Commanding Officer of all US forces in the Dominican Republic (left). Major General Robert York, Commander of the US Army 82nd Airborne Division (right). (US Army Archives)

Phase 2: Advance to the Ozama River

After landing, York and Masterson met aboard USS *Boxer* to plan their next move. To trap the Constitutionalists in the city's Ciudad Nueva district, they envisioned the 82nd Airborne Division moving from the airport to Duarte Bridge (which spanned the Ozama River and led into Santo Domingo), while the marines held the left flank and the Loyalists the centre. At dawn on 30 April the 1st Battalion, 508th Infantry advanced along the San Isidro Highway to secure the bridge's eastern approach.

Two 82nd Airborne Division paratroopers at a checkpoint at Duarte Bridge with a MUTT M151 vehicle armed with a recoilless rifle. (US Army Archives)

A motorised column of paratroopers from the 82nd Airborne Division moving through the streets of Santo Domingo to create the security corridor with the ISZ. (US Army Archives)

Men of Company C crossed and established a six-block beachhead encompassing the city's main power station. Simultaneously, 1st Battalion, 505th Infantry established a perimeter around the field and sent patrols into the adjacent countryside. The CEFA troops had orders to transfer their positions to the Americans and they never abandoned their positions. When the Americans arrived at the Duarte Bridge, they took over the positions of the CEFA troops on both sides of the bridge.

Phase 3: Closing the Gap and Establishment of the Line of Communications

The rebels were able to move freely through this gap and distribute weapons throughout the city. York secured approval for four more battalions to close the gap, but Johnson worried another unilateral move would resemble the 1956 Soviet invasion of Hungary, further damaging OAS relations. Nevertheless, Operation Power Pack II began, which sent emergency medical supplies, equipment, and units, including a field hospital and a medical battalion from Fort Bragg, which was carried out between noon and midnight on 1 May.

Johnson instructed Wheeler to resolve the situation quickly. Wheeler then appointed Lieutenant General Bruce Palmer, Jr., who was serving as Army Deputy Chief of Staff for Operations, as Commanding General, United States Forces Dominican Republic to replace York. On 1 May, Palmer received command of XVIII Airborne Corps; he now had over 24,000 troops at his disposal. Wheeler also emphasised that the operation's success depended on close cooperation with Ambassador Bennett.

After arriving on the island, Palmer realised the rebels were throughout the city while the troops from San Isidro were only in the Fair sector and the area near the National Palace, blocks from the American Embassy, and these were Army troops from the *Enriquillo* Battalion. Palmer hoped to force the two factions to seek a negotiated solution. On 1 May Palmer briefed the JCS on this plan and ordered York to reconnoitre the 2.5 kilometres from the Duarte Bridge to the ISZ to determine the feasibility of closing the gap and opening an American controlled corridor linking the Army and Marine forces. Two platoons from Company C, 1-508 Infantry completed the mission, but took seven casualties. Nevertheless, the reconnaissance proved the gap could be closed. Before proceeding, Johnson wanted the plan cleared with the OAS. The following day Palmer met with OAS Secretary General José Mora and a special committee who gave their permission after a brief and cordial discussion. On the following day, Operation Power Pack III was carried out, delivering more equipment from the US to San Isidro AFB and finally on 3 May Operation Power Pack IV was done.

On 3 May at midnight, three American infantry battalions left Duarte Bridge, leapfrogging toward the marines within the ISZ whom they contacted at 1:12 am. By moving at night and avoiding known concentrations of rebel forces, the 82nd Airborne Division established a four-block-wide line of communications. Palmer's plan was to establish a route for American supplies and communications through the city by creating a security corridor connecting the ISZ with Duarte Bridge. This cut Santo Domingo in two parts, with 80 percent of the rebels in their Ciudad Nueva stronghold.

During the four POWER PACK operations, completed on 5 May, USAF transported a total of 12,000 troops and 7,500 tons of cargo. This effort took 915 sorties, 596 by TAC C-130s, 227 by MATS C-130s and 92 by C-124s. Also, at least 19 Fairchild C-119 Flying

US Marines patrolling the streets of the ISZ in Santo Domingo (left). Paratroopers with an M274 Mule armed with a recoilless rifle in Santo Domingo (right). Note the then-new M16 assault rifles being carried by troops in both photographs. (USMC & US Army Archives)

The three types of troop and cargo transport aircraft used by the USAF in Operation Power Pack: Lockheed C-130E Hercules (top left), Douglas C-124C Globemaster II (top right) and Fairchild C-119 Flying Boxcar (bottom). (USAF Archives)

Boxcar aircraft were used to transport heavy equipment. In six-plus days almost 16,000 troops and about 14,000 tons of materiel and supplies were airlifted between the United States and the Dominican Republic, the largest sustained US troop airlift ever accomplished up to that time. Almost 1,500 sorties involving 181 C-130s and 23 C-124s were flown under difficult weather and airfield conditions without a single mishap.

The contingency plan for operations in the Dominican Republic provided for the deployment of fighter and reconnaissance aircraft, which were deployed to Ramey AFB in Puerto Rico on 2 May. The fighter unit consisted of 18 North American F-100D Super Sabre fighters with four spares, from the 354th Tactical Fighter Wing (TFW), which took off from Myrtle Beach AFB in South Carolina, refuelled by Boeing KC-135 Stratotanker aircraft, to reach Puerto Rico. They flew a total of 313 sorties in 594 hours patrolling the Dominican skies just in case Cuban MiGs were deployed to help the rebels. They returned to their base in the US on 28 May. Six USAF 363th Tactical Reconnaissance Wing (TRW) McDonnell RF-

USAF fighters and reconnaissance aircraft deployed to Ramey AFB in Puerto Rico during Operation Power Pack in the Dominican Republic: 354th TFW North American F-100D Super Sabres (top left), 363th TRW McDonnell RF-101C Voodoos (top right), Douglas RB-66C Destroyers (bottom left) and 319th FIS Lockheed F-104E Starfighters, which replaced the F-100Ds. (USAF Archives via Albert Grandolini)

101C Voodoo and three Douglas RB-66C Destroyer aircraft were deployed to Ramey AFB also on 2 May as a reconnaissance element. The Voodoos carried out several photoreconnaissance sorties over Santo Domingo and accurate maps of the city were made with the pictures taken. In the case of the RB-66Cs, they were used to monitor the rebel radio communications. When the F-100s returned to their bases, 12 Lockheed F-104E Starfighter interceptors from the 319th Fighter Interceptor Squadron (FIS) based in Homestead, Florida were sent to Ramey Air Base in the event that supply flights to the Dominican Republic could be affected by Cuban MiGs. The USAF F-104s remained at Ramey until 3 June.

Special Air Warfare units also saw service in the Dominican Republic. The USAF sent two Douglas C-47s equipped with powerful loudspeakers for psywar duties, together with two Fairchild C-123 Providers and two Helio U-10A Couriers. None of these planes were lost due to enemy fire, although they were hit by rebel fire several times.

American Peacekeeping

By 4 May 1965 Palmer had overseen the largest buildup of US forces in Latin America (nearly 24,000 at peak strength) and established an air bridge between Pope AFB and San Isidro Airfield. The additional forces deployed included the 82nd Airborne Division's two remaining brigades, 5th Logistics Command, 15th Field Hospital, 503rd Military Police Battalion, 50th Signal Battalion, 218th Military Intelligence Battalion, 42nd Civil Affairs Company, and elements of the 519th Military Intelligence Battalion, 1st Psychological Warfare Battalion, and 7th Special Forces Group. From 4 to 23 May, the United States military conducted unilateral peacekeeping operations. The rebels had the weapons they needed and plenty of ammunition obtained from the Ozama Fortress. Colonel Benoit was no longer president of the junta; General Imbert Barrera was appointed and volunteered. Under the presence of American forces, the OAS helped negotiate a ceasefire agreement, signed by General Imbert and Colonel Francisco Caamaño Deñó, representing the Loyalist and Constitutionalist factions, respectively.

Despite sporadic sniping, which accounted for the majority of American casualties, US forces had little difficulty conducting peacekeeping and garrison duties. No major engagements erupted between Loyalist and Constitutionalist forces until 13 May when Loyalist General Antonio Imbert Barrera launched an eight-day offensive called Operation Clean-up to eliminate rebel resistance north of the line of communications. Ambassador Bennett lodged an official complaint with the OAS, but Imbert's actions ultimately aided the American cause by allowing the United States to play the role of the neutral. The unilateral American phase of the intervention ended when the OAS established the IAPF.

From left to right, USAF Special Air Warfare Douglas C-47, Fairchild C-123 and Helio U-10A Courier operated during the Dominican Crisis in 1965. (Ralf Manteufel & USAF Archives)

Transition and US Departure

To ensure a peaceful transition the rebel-occupied Ciudad Nueva district needed to be disarmed and demilitarised. Operations to accomplish this occurred in two phases. First, on 13–14 October, by agreement with García-Godoy and the Constitutionalists, military police and troops from the 82nd Airborne Division evacuated most rebel military forces. The second phase took place on 25 October and occurred without the full approval of García-Godoy, who was being indecisive. During this phase IAPF forces comprised of elements of the 82nd Airborne Division conducted a sweep south across the district from positions along the line of communications. Meanwhile, the Latin American battalions assumed blocking positions to seal the district's western approaches. The operation proceeded without incident and the IAPF removed the remaining rebels, located several arms caches, and uncovered numerous incriminating communist documents. Elements of the 82nd Airborne Division remained in Ciudad Nueva until 1 November and a company of soldiers from 1st Battalion, 505th Infantry remained to occupy the city's power plant and the Duarte Bridge.

The last major confrontation occurred on 19 December at 09:00 AM in Santiago when 300 Loyalists attacked 150 Constitutionalists under Caamaño as they departed a mass held for the slain Colonel Fernández Domínguez. The gun battle raged for five hours until a company of American soldiers interposed themselves between the factions, negotiated the release of 15 Americans, and allowed both sides to disengage. In the first months of 1966 military chiefs of both sides agreed to accept diplomatic postings overseas. Wessin refused to go into exile and tried to carry out a coup d'état, but the American soldiers in San Isidro prevented him, and put him on a plane to Panama. The agreement was that all rebel and loyal soldiers would accept diplomatic positions. In the presidential elections on 1 June 1966, Joaquín Balaguer won 57 percent of the vote, defeating Juan Bosch. Both men remained active in the Dominican political scene through the 1990s, although Bosch never again held public office.

On 21 September 1966, after overseeing a peaceful transfer of power to Balaguer, the last American forces departed. Nearly 24,000 soldiers and marines had been deployed to the island, of whom 27 were killed and 172 wounded. US military forces succeeded in enabling the administration to achieve its goals of protecting the lives of Americans, restoring peace and political stability in the Dominican Republic, and conducting multi-national operations with their Latin American counterparts as part of the IAPF.

APPENDICES

Appendix I
Psyops Operations in the Dominican Republic in 1965 During Operation Power Pack

Lieutenant Colonel Wallace J. Moulis, Commanding Officer of the 1st PSYWAR (Psychological Warfare) Battalion, in charge of the psychological operations in the Dominican Republic during Operation Power Pack in 1965 reported that on the afternoon of 1 May, in response to a request from Mr. Hewson A. Ryan, United States Information Agency (USIA) Director, the 1st PSYWAR Battalion at Fort Bragg, North Carolina, was directed to dispatch the first elements of the Army's psychological warfare effort in support of the operation directed by the United States Information Service (USIS).

Operational elements of the 1st PSYWAR Company (Field Army), reinforced with radio broadcast and light, mobile audiovisual teams, as well as language experts, were readied for a midnight departure. A liaison officer was dispatched to join Ryan with the mission of coordinating military support and assisting the overall operation in any way possible. The battalion's van-mounted radio was prepared to follow shortly by heavy airlift.

Almost before the roar of their aircraft had left their ears, the radio teams with Ray Aylor, *Voice of America* radio engineer, were repairing a 1,000-watt transmitter to begin relaying *Voice of America* transmission from Greenville, North Carolina. Production of leaflets by mimeograph began even before the arrival of light, mobile presses. Loudspeakers took positions along the Ozama River to bring the voice of the United States to the people.

Bert H. Cooper Jr. stated that the most significant organisational achievement of the Dominican operation in the area of communications was the combining of civilian and military talents by the USIA and the Army's 1st PSYWAR Battalion (later to become the 1st PSYOP [Psychological Operations] Battalion). He called it a classic case of successful interagency cooperation in a crisis situation. In fact, the USIA later presented the 1st PSYWAR Battalion with its Award for Distinguished Service, its highest commendation. The citation read:

> United States Information Agency
> Award for Distinguished Service.
> Presented to the
>
> First Psychological Warfare Battalion, United States Army
>
> In recognition of outstanding support and assistance to the United States Information Service in the Dominican Republic during the month of May 1965.
>
> Washington D.C.
> 15 June 1965
> Carl T. Rowan
> Director

Each battalion member received a personal letter of commendation from their commander.

The PSYWAR personnel and equipment arrived in San Isidro AFB on 2 May, and just three days later they started broadcasting. The USIA staff in the Dominican Republic was familiar with the country and had the professional and language skills. However, they lacked the communications equipment and facilities that the Army could supply and the military lacked language skills. This was attested to in part by correspondence from Specialist Dave Hagen who was assigned to the 1st PSYWAR Battalion as a broadcast specialist. He mentioned that he was one of eight or nine GI's running a portable radio station called the *Voice of the Security Zone* that went on the air on 5 May.

Because the main government radio station was in rebel hands, Hagen and his team had to broadcast from a small station in the

Four members of the US Army's 1st PSYWAR Battalion using loudspeakers mounted on a MUTT M151, making the population aware of the reasons for the American presence in Santo Domingo. Note the M14 rifle carried by the soldier sitting in the rear of the jeep. (US Army Archives via Albert Grandolini)

1st PSYWAR Battalion troops in front of the Radio Broadcast Van in Santo Domingo (right). (US Army Archives via Albert Grandolini)

1st PSYWAR Battalion personnel handing in a propaganda leaflet to a civilian in Santo Domingo (top left); posters explaining the dangers of communism were widely distributed in the capital (top right); two US paratroopers show a 1J4 poster against the American presence in Santo Domingo (bottom left); 1st PSYWAR Battalion personnel distributing newspapers on board a US Army Dodge M35 truck surrounded by civilians in a Santo Domingo street. (US Army Archives)

1st PSYWAR Battalion Specialist Dave Hagen (left). Part of the US Army radio equipment in semi-trailers brought to Santo Domingo (right). (US Army Archives)

countryside. They drove west from San Isidro Air Base several miles and turned off the main road into a residential area before they reached the Ozama River and the Duarte Bridge (a scene of heavy fighting). In this residential area they arrived at a one-acre field with a standing AM radio broadcast tower and a small cement building. The building was empty and there were no signs of any combat in the area. This building was about 10' x 10' which was the perfect size for an AM radio transmitter and its associated equipment. There were no studio facilities in the area. They set up their equipment and used the standing antenna. Overall, they had a generator, studio truck, transmitter truck, communications truck, and the antenna tuning truck.

Their unit had a complete radio station in their five trucks. They broadcast their own programming rather than just rebroadcasting *Voice of America*. The 1st PSYWAR Battalion consisted of three groups: RB (radio broadcast), Loudspeaker, and Leaflets. They also had a unit for support. All were commanded by Lieutenant Colonel Wallace Moulis. Their RB group was commanded by Captain William Perry. They also had two lieutenants, Williams and Pojmanski, two master sergeants, Tokifuji and Fewles, and three specialists. They were in a war zone and thus slept with their weapons nearby. When things got quiet, they tried to win the 'hearts and minds' of local children by playing baseball with them and many had mitts and softballs.

Was the radio station successful? Hagen added they were trying to let people know what was happening and that American troops had established a buffer zone between three warring factions. They also wanted to let them know that they were their friends. They saw both civilians and military listening to them on portable radios. Kids hung around the radio station and women brought them coffee in the morning. They seemed to be well liked. Of course, they were heavily armed and brought a sense of security to the area of Santo Domingo that they were in. At the time, it appeared that their messages helped to end the fighting. Reports in the years following the American 'intervention' contended that they were simply trying to stop the spread of communism. That was true, but they also helped to end a civil war.

Latin American specialists working for the USIS in Santo Domingo could have performed those tasks except that their printing and broadcast equipment were located in buildings then controlled by the rebels.

On 4 May they were ready to start broadcasting to the Dominican Republic. Hagen was the only announcer (broadcast specialist) with the 4th RB team and did not speak Spanish so they did not start actual broadcasts until 5 May when an employee of the USIA arrived. Their *Voice of the Security Zone* hit the AM airwaves and was powerful enough to be picked up in the surrounding countryside. He was told their broadcasting explained to the population the positive side of the intervention, and the need to restore order and democracy. Civilian specialists wrote scripts and other forms of propaganda under the direction of Ryan, associate director of the

American soldiers of the PSYWAR Company playing baseball with Dominican children under the watchful eye of numerous onlookers. (Albert Grandolini Archives)

DOMINICANOS ESTE ES SU PAÍS

¡ NO SE DEJEN ENGAÑAR POR LOS COMUNISTAS !

Two examples of political propaganda: A poster of the communist-oriented 14 June Movement (1J4) (left) and a leaflet distributed by Americans that says: 'Dominicans, this is your country. Don't be fooled by the communists' (right). (US Army Archives)

A US Army PSYWAR Battalion 5-ton M39 truck followed by a Dodge M35 and an M151 MUTT carrying food for the needy civilian population (left). Thousands of people received food from American troops in Santo Domingo (right). (Albert Grandolini Archives)

American soldiers distributing food and supplies to Dominican civilians in Santo Domingo. (Albert Grandolini Archives)

USIA. Their team was not involved with any propaganda planning and was simply tasked with keeping the radio station on the air.

The 1st PSYWAR Company radio broadcast equipment consisted of three truck mounted modules and two semi-trailers. The modules contained a communications unit (teletype and voice), an antenna tuning unit, and a power generator. The semis pulled a studio trailer and a transmitter trailer. When the rest of the 1st Psychological Warfare Battalion arrived in the Dominican Republic between 3 and 7 May, it brought with it mobile printing presses and loudspeaker units.

Within a week the first pamphlet drop was made over Santo Domingo using two Air Force C-47s. One report stated that by the end of May leaflets were being printed at a rate of 70,000 per day. The printing facilities were in a different location than their broadcasting station so Hagen did not see any of the leaflets. None were air dropped in their area.

Later, two additional transmitters were added to the network. The Army conducted 600 hours of loudspeaker operations, and broadcast over 900 hours of in-country programs. In addition, they relayed the *Voice of America* broadcasts for 35 days.

There was a lively propaganda war on the airwaves of the Dominican Republic. The history of the 193rd USAF Special Operation Wing mentioned that the efforts of US military forces, operating alongside Dominican Republic governmental troops, were hindered by a rebel-operated radio station, which continually broadcast information to resistance forces.

US PSYWAR radio was able to monitor and answer rebel radio diatribes about *El Imperialismo Yanqui* (Yankee Imperialism) and put out the first newspaper since the outbreak of the revolt.

On the other hand, Carl Black was a radioman aboard the US Navy destroyer DD-844 USS *Perry*. The ship was assigned to the naval battle group sent to the Dominican Republic. He mentioned that initially they were in the destroyer screen closest to shore off Santo Domingo. They were notified that an AM radio station had fallen into the hands of the rebels and they were given its frequency and instructed to jam it. Since they had an AM transceiver with over twice the output power of the radio station, they came up on their frequency with a deliberately bad transmitter setup and keyed the transmitter. This 'bad setup' caused the transmitter to create a variable frequency audio tone osculating in the audio range centred

Rebel Radio Santo Domingo's transmissions were jammed by the powerful radio equipment of the destroyer DD-844 USS *Perry*. (US Navy Archives)

on their frequency. They maintained this until they were notified that the radio station was back in government hands.

Some of the most important clandestine operations during the intervention attempted to silence *Radio Santo Domingo* (RSD). Although a poor people by US standards, virtually every Dominican family owned a radio and, because of the country's high illiteracy rate, relied on it heavily for information. RSD, with 'numerous outlets, studios, and transmitter sites', was the country's national station, capable of being heard throughout the island. In the hands of the rebels, the station became a powerful propaganda weapon, in fact, the biggest thorn in the side of the Americans. Langley received a telephone call from a CIA agent with a blunt message: 'The difference in Santo Domingo', the agent shouted, 'lies in that radio station. If the rebels continue their propaganda, they will take over the entire country. The radio must be silenced!'.

The problem was that nothing seemed to work. Naval vessels offshore and the Army Security Agency both tried to jam RSD broadcasts, but neither had powerful enough equipment to interfere more than temporarily with the broadcasting range of a commercial station. On 8 and 10 May, Special Forces teams mounted successful air assault operations against RSD transmitter sites at Alto Bandero and La Vega, thereby reducing the effectiveness of RSD broadcasts in those and surrounding areas. The day after the Special Forces seized the La Vega transmitter, a team of paratroopers and Green Berets slipped into the north and severed telecommunication lines. The operation failed to shut down the radio station, but it did disrupt the telephone system used by the rebels for tactical purposes. By 13 May, Palmer had had enough and requested permission from Washington to mount an overt military operation against RSD. Finally, during *Operacion Limpieza*, the Government of National Reconstruction captured Radio Santo Domingo.

The insurgents were not above the using tragic American accidents and incidents as anti-American propaganda. Private First Class Bill Quigley assigned to the 307th Medical Battalion near the Duarte Bridge mentioned that a US trooper accidentally killed a 10-year-old Dominican shoeshine boy when his .45 calibre pistol discharged while he was using it to remove the cap from a bottle of Coca Cola. The body was held in a building next to the aid station until the family claimed it. Eventually, a Dominican man came for the body, claiming to be an uncle. Unit officers suspected that the 'uncle' was really a rebel who wanted to parade the body through the streets as anti-American propaganda. Army Intelligence assigned a warrant officer to interrogate the alleged uncle. After questioning, he confessed that he was not a relative. He was a member of Colonel Caamaño's rebel forces and his mission was to collect the boy's body for propaganda purposes. He was immediately turned over to the *Policia Nacional* and probably never heard from again.

Specialist Fourth Class Don Sebastian was a member of the 82nd Airborne who arrived in the Dominican Republic on day two of the invasion. He said that he was called to the headquarters of General Robert York; Commander of the 82nd Airborne Division shortly after the division took some losses at the battle of the Duarte Bridge. The Dominican Popular Movement, a small communist party force had distributed Molotov cocktails to the crowds, and the rebel military, well supplied with mortars, machine guns, bazookas and small arms were defending the Duarte Bridge. Both the pro and anti-Government forces wore the same uniform and it was impossible to distinguish friend from foe.

Don said he was called to headquarters by General York and found two finance officers and a jeep full of shopping bags containing US$100 bills. His orders were to hand out banknotes to individuals near the bridge. Don had no idea why he was given that mission but believes it was to empty the enemy ranks of fighters. When word got out that the Americans were giving out US$100 bills, Dominican civilians came from everywhere, and many of them were young men of military age who might have been carrying rifles just minutes earlier. Could this have been a ploy to clear the area of Dominicans and reduce collateral damage?

In fact, it was not just the Army that ran a psychological operations radio station. The Navy was also involved. In late 1964 Navy Captain George Dixon became Manager of *Project Jenny*, the US Navy operation to use aircraft to broadcast radio in support of psychological operations. He met with the Radio Corporation of America (RCA) concerning the feasibility of using an aircraft as a radio broadcasting platform. Although dubious, RCA agreed to provide equipment and technical expertise. The aircraft configuration and technical work was performed by Navy enlisted personnel.

The first Blue Eagle aircraft was constructed in January 1965 using a Lockheed NC-121J Super Constellation shell. *Blue Eagle I* was the first project aircraft and configured to do AM, FM, and SW radio broadcast missions. A crew of naval officers and enlisted personnel

US Navy Lockheed NC-121J Super Constellation called *Blue Eagle I*. (US Navy Archives)

was selected. Operational and flight training began in July 1965. In September 1965 *Blue Eagle I* was ordered to Naval Air Station Roosevelt Roads in Puerto Rico to fly radio missions in support of US PSYOP efforts in the Dominican Republic. *Blue Eagle I* was on station for approximately two weeks and then returned to Andrews AFB. The aircraft was sent to Vietnam shortly afterwards where it broadcast Armed Forces Vietnam Network (AFVN) radio from 1965–1967 and earned the nickname *Danang Dirty Bird.* A year later the Air Force was given the assignment of airborne psychological operations and it has continued that mission ever since.

Details of the Navy's use of aircraft as propaganda platforms were revealed by Electronics Technician Second Class Chuck Hammond who was stationed at the Anacostia Naval Air Base from mid-1963 to November 1966. Chuck was assigned directly to Chief of Naval Operations for special assignments. He mentioned that he was assigned to the US Naval Security Station, Washington DC in November 1963 after Electronics Technician "A" School in San Francisco. They worked for the Chief of Naval Operations as a mobile communications unit and most of their assignments were temporary additional duty to some other location. The unit was stationed at the old Anacostia Naval Air Station just north of Boling Air Force Base in south-west Washington. All that was there at that time were empty hangars. They stored all of the communications equipment in those hangars except for any cryptologist gear. In early 1965 they began testing radio broadcasting from a Navy Douglas R5D aircraft. The equipment that they had in their possession at the time was two RCA TR-22 video tape recorders. They were the first solid-state recorders and used a 2-inch tape.

On about 12 May they were sent to Andrews Air Force base and deployed to Roosevelt Roads Air Base in Puerto Rico. On board the plane were the two video tape recorders and a 55-kilowatt diesel generator to provide power to them. They initially had RCA technicians come in and train them on-site. Their job was to maintain the recorders as the plane flew over the Dominican Republic and broadcast a TV signal. He mentioned that he did not know what they broadcast since it was all in Spanish but it was surely a propaganda message. They landed in Santo Domingo a few times and returned to Washington after two to three weeks. When they returned a Super Constellation equipped similarly to their plane was at Andrews AFB and a member of their unit was working on it.

Television sets were at a premium in the Dominican Republic so the United States sent a plane full of 13-inch black and white TV sets to be distributed to the people so they could watch what they were broadcasting.

A US Navy Douglas R5D (left). An RCA TR-22 Video Tape Recorder (right). (US Navy Archives)

Radioman Chief Petty Officer Steve Robbins, United States Navy, remembered it a bit differently. He just wanted to set the record straight on *Blue Eagle I*. To the best of his memory, *Blue Eagle I* deployed to Naval Air Station Roosevelt Roads to provide airborne broadcast services for the Dominican Republic, but for whatever reason never actually conducted any broadcast operations.

Hewson A. Ryan, Associate Director USIA (Policy and Plans) was assigned the task of coordinating all PSYOP in the Dominican Republic. He had been involved in the Cuban missile crisis and as a result was aware of the need for air delivery of leaflets, radio and loudspeaker broadcasts. Cooper said that to assist him, the Army sent the entire 1st PSYWAR Battalion to Santo Domingo from Fort Bragg, North Carolina, in early May. A temporary base of operations was set up in the home of the Public Affairs Officer near the American Embassy. The battalion soon moved into a nearby school building. The Army supplied radio transmitters, mobile presses, multilith machines, loudspeaker trucks, and aircraft for leaflet and loudspeaker operations. Cooper mentioned that the working relationships were particularly good and the military-civilian mix worked extremely well. Most of the battalion and the heavy equipment returned to Fort Bragg by June. At that time, the priority changed from psychological operations to civil affairs and nation-building support.

At the height of the operation there were some problems with both the hostile press and with the OAS. There was basic agreement among US policymakers that the Dominican Republic should not be permitted to become 'a second Cuba'. However, beyond that point, there was a wide divergence of opinion as to the steps which should be taken by the US government and about the nature and extent of communist influence in the Dominican situation. It was the opinion of the American ambassador and most US representatives in the country that a rebel victory would open the way for a communist seizure of the government in the immediate or near future.

The Department of State, which had responsibility for determining national policy objectives and strategies in the Dominican Republic, exercised overall supervision of all US activity in the country. In several instances the State Department differed with US representatives in Santo Domingo over certain operations. For example, when a visiting delegation of OAS representatives complained that the leaflets being dropped from US planes contained propaganda material in support of the Loyalist military junta, the State Department asked that leaflet drops by military aircraft be halted. State also objected to the Army's interrogation of Dominicans held by US forces for investigation and intelligence purposes.

Leaflets bearing pictures of Presidents John F. Kennedy and Lyndon B. Johnson and pamphlets extolling the virtues of the OAS and the evils of communism became standard, if innocuous fare. Some propaganda, however, was blatantly false, as USIS officials tried to convince the population that the intervention was a benevolent undertaking. One of the battalion's after-action reports listed among the USIS-imposed propaganda themes such fictions as 'the landing was made for peaceful and humanitarian ends', and the 'U S government supports neither side nor has it given military aid to either faction'.

Some examples of the leaflets' text (the originals were all in Spanish) were:

> The forces of law and order are here for the protection and good of all Dominicans. Laws and additional precautions are necessary in time of war. Dominicans, this is your country. Do not be fooled by the communists
>
> The United States will give its full support to the work of the OAS and never vary from its commitment to preserve the right of all free peoples of this hemisphere to follow their own path without falling victim to the international conspiracy from wherever it comes … Lyndon B. Johnson.
>
> 3 May 1965
> Dominican citizens:
> This is the TRUTH, the TRUTH about the American landing.
> The landing was made only for peaceful and humanitarian purposes.
> The landing was made only when the Dominican civil and military forces lost the ability to protect the lives of North American citizens and those of other nations.
> The United States government does not support any faction nor has it lent military aid or materials to any faction.
> The United States government only advocates the freedom and welfare of the Dominican people within a constitutional framework.
> The United States government has collaborated with the Red Cross to provide emergency aid all the Dominicans affected by the current crisis.
> The United States government is lending its entire support to the negotiations by the Organization of American States to solve the crisis.
> Liberty Yes!
> Communism No!

Army PSYWAR operators produced and distributed over two and a half million printed propaganda items. It seems apparent that the leaflets were dropped for a short period and probably only in and around the capitol city of Santo Domingo.

The poor performance of the Army Public Affairs Officers (PAO) and the admitted lack of the ability to run a fair and balanced briefing was the start of the adversarial attitude between the Army and the press that came to a head in Vietnam. In their defence, the PAOs were forced to parrot the line that the United States was neutral and simply trying to bring peace to a divided nation, when it was clear that the military action was taken rid the Dominican Republic of a movement that was perceived as communist inspired.

The PSYOP group was handed a difficult role because they did not have a good intelligence feed and had to use what came from the embassy and Washington DC. They had to parrot the official line. The American Ambassador was noted for being close to the old Trujillo crowd including the rich and the corrupt military leadership. Most of the military and the civilian population, constituting the so-called Rebel or Constitutional faction, did not want yet another military coup and leadership by the corrupt generals. Communism was used as an excuse to invade, but much later it was discovered by intelligence sources that they never found evidence of significant communist influence among the Constitutionalists. They continued to say that the United States of America was neutral while funding the junta and allowing it to move through the 'disarmed corridor'.

There were not really any good solutions: Juan Bosch was an ineffective administrator and leader; General Trujillo had eliminated any potential leaders and corrupted the influential and rich; arranging for Joaquín Balaguer to win elections was probably the best of the poor choices for ending the situation. Unfortunately, he continued the corruption and did nothing for the development of the country or to help the general population.

Two posters appealing to Dominicans to freedom with the pious image of the Virgin Mary (left) and to reject enslaving communism (right). (Open Source)

Meanwhile, the US Special Forces had two missions. The overt mission was to deliver food with choppers to various locations. The second mission had small groups tucked away at key points around the country with heavy firepower where they could control the major roads. They were aware of about six such locations.

The State Department seems to have been out of step with the USIA and the military, interfering with a complex operation. This caused confusion among personnel and led to mixed messages being sent to the enemy. The State Department also seems to have disagreed with the CIA's conclusion of a strong communist influence in the Dominican Republic. Like Vietnam, they had one segment of the government treating the action as a civil war while another treated it as a communist insurrection. The lack of a strong PSYOP effort was commented upon by Captain James B. Oerding who spent 22 days in-country at the height of the fighting as a team leader in the 7th Special Forces Group. He mentioned that during his 22 days in the Dominican Republic, he never saw any indication of PSYOP activities, no leaflets, no posters, no newspapers, no loudspeakers, nothing. However, the Radio Station in Santo Domingo, after it was recaptured was used for PSYOP and other broadcasts.

US Army Specialist Fifth Class Bill Cohune gave more details about the PSYOP campaign. He was drafted September 1963 and assigned to the 1st PSYWAR Battalion Fort Bragg, North Carolina in January 1964. In April 1965, his entire unit including the Printing Platoon, Radio Broadcast Platoon, and the graphic artist contingent was deployed to Santo Domingo. Bill was assigned to the graphics group as a photographer with Colonel Moulis's headquarters group encamped near the US Embassy in Santo Domingo. The graphic group was assigned the task of developing leaflet and poster ideas that would depict the positive sides of the US involvement and motivate the Dominican people to reject the rebels. The reaction from the population was generally positive. Bill mentioned that his specific tasks were to take pictures of subjects that could be used in the leaflets, and then to take pictures of the distribution of the leaflets and posters. He also made a number of helicopter leaflet drops in various areas of Santo Domingo.

His equipment was a Pentax SLR camera for colour slides, which were all retained by the headquarters, and a speed Graflex press camera with a Polaroid pack for proofs and confirmations. The final black and white films were processed by a technician in another group, as the PSYWAR battalion did not have mobile dark room capabilities. He was only allowed to keep some of the proofs.

A newspaper was printed in support of the Army operation by the USIS starting 5 May and 75,000 copies per issue were printed in Miami, Florida, and forwarded to the Dominican Republic for dissemination. At the same time, to help support the Army printing on mobile presses, posters and pamphlets were printed by the USIA plant in Mexico City.

Captain Blaine Revis who commanded the 19th PSYOP Company from June 1964 to August 1965 reported about deploying his troops to the Dominican Republic during Operation Power Pack. He stated that they sent two loudspeaker teams augmented with two Spanish-speaking linguists and a print section (a 3/4-ton truck with pod). They flew into San Isidro on D+1 on a C-47 Skytrain and a C-119 Flying Boxcar. The C-47 was hit by three rounds of small arms fire on landing approach. Their assigned sector was rather agrarian and soon quiet and compliant. He attributed that to some extent to the rice and beans and odd C-rations that they gave out to the people, along with Latin music that they played on the loudspeakers. The 82nd Airborne Division had a roving medical team that was well received among the local populace.

Some problems that were identified were the time it took to receive supplies from the United States, the obsolescence of some of the equipment, the lack of good maps and intelligence, and the lack of Spanish-trained linguists. This affected not only the radio operations, but also the printing operations where errors were made due to the lack of knowledge of the language.

There was also enemy propaganda. The revolutionaries also prepared some posters. In one of them, a grotesque crazed US Marine coming ashore holding his rifle in such a way that it was plain that he was about to bayonet the innocent viewer. In the background were American ships and aircraft. In another one, an armed American soldier clearly marked with USA on his helmet while an unseen enemy used his rifle (perhaps implying a sniper or perhaps the whole Dominican population) to shoot the hated Yankee.

Appendix II

Table 14: Dominican Armed Forces ranks[1]

Army Officers	Air Force Officers	Navy Officers
Teniente General (Lieutenant General)	*Teniente General* (Lieutenant General)	*Almirante* (Admiral)
Mayor General (Major General)	*Mayor General* (Major General)	*Vice Almirante* (Vice Admiral)
General de Brigada (Brigadier General)	*General de Brigada* (Brigadier General)	*Contralmirante* (Rear Admiral)
Coronel (Colonel)	*Coronel* (Colonel)	*Capitán de Navío* (Ship Captain)
Teniente Coronel (Lieutenant Colonel)	*Teniente Coronel* (Lieutenant Colonel)	*Capitán de Fragata* (Frigate Captain)
Mayor (Major)	*Mayor* (Major)	*Capitán de Corbeta* (Corvette Captain)
Capitán (Captain)	*Capitán* (Captain)	*Teniente de Navío* (Ship Lieutenant)
Primer Teniente (First Lieutenant)	*Primer Teniente* (First Lieutenant)	*Teninete de Fragata* (Frigate Lieutenant)
Segundo Teniente (Second Lieutenant)	*Segundo Teniente* (Second Lieutenant)	*Teniente de Corbeta* (Corvette Lieutenant)
Military Academy	**Air Force Academy AFA**	**Naval Academy**
Cadete 4to Año (4th Year Cadet)	*Cadete 4to Año AFA* (4th Year Cadet)	*Guardiamarina 4to Año* (4th Year Midshipman)
Cadete 3er Año (3rd Year Cadet)	*Cadete 3er Año AFA* (3rd Year Cadet)	*Guardiamarina 3er Año* (3rd Year Midshipman)
Cadete 2do Año (2nd Year Cadet)	*Cadete 2do Año AFA* (2nd Year Cadet)	*Guardiamarina 2do Año* (2nd Year Midshipman)
Cadete 1er Año (1st Year Cadet)	*Cadete 1er Año AFA* (1st Year Cadet)	*Guardiamarina 1er Año* (1st Year Midshipman)
Army NCOs	**Air Force NCOs**	**Navy NCOs**
Subteniente III (III Sub-Lieutenant)	*Sargento Mayor* (Major Sergeant)	*Subteniente III* (III Sub-Lieutenant)
Subteniente II (II Sub-Lieutenant)	*Sargento* (Sergeant)	*Subteniente II* (II Sub-Lieutenant)
Subteniente I (I Sub-Lieutenant)	–	*Subteniente I* (I Sub-Lieutenant)
Sargento Mayor (Major Sergeant)	–	*Sargento Mayor* (Major Sergeant)
Sargento (Sergeant)	–	*Sargento* (Sergeant)
Army Enlisted	**Air Force Enlisted**	**Navy Enlisted**
Cabo (Corporal)	*Cabo* (Corporal)	*Cabo* (Corporal)
Raso (Conscript/Private)	*Raso* (Conscript/Private)	*Marinero* (Sailor)
–	–	*Grumete* (Grummet)

Table 15: Dominican National Police ranks[2]

General Officers	Senior Officers	Junior Officers	NCOs	Enlisted	Police Students
Mayor General (Major General)	*Coronel* (Colonel)	*Capitán* (Captain)	*Sargento Mayor* (Major Sergeant)	*Sargento* (Sergeant)	*Cadete* (Cadet)
General (General)	*Teniente Coronel* (Lieutenant Colonel)	*Primer Teniente* (1st Lieutenant)	–	*Cabo* (Corporal)	*Conscripto* (Conscript)
–	*Mayor* (Major)	*Segundo Teniente* (2nd Lieutenant)	–	*Raso* (Private)	–

Table 16: US Armed Forces ranks[3]

Army	Marine Corps	Navy	Air Force
General of the Army (*)	N/A	Fleet Admiral (*)	General of the Air Force (*)
General	General	Admiral	General
Lieutenant General	Lieutenant General	Vice Admiral	Lieutenant General
Major General	Major General	Rear Admiral – Upper Half	Major General
Brigadier General	Brigadier General	Rear Admiral – Lower Half	Brigadier General
Colonel	Colonel	Captain	Colonel
Lieutenant Colonel	Lieutenant Colonel	Commander	Lieutenant Colonel
Major	Major	Lieutenant Commander	Major
Captain	Captain	Lieutenant	Captain
First Lieutenant	First Lieutenant	Lieutenant Junior Grade	First Lieutenant
Second Lieutenant	Second Lieutenant	Ensign	Second Lieutenant
Chief Warrant Officer 5	Chief Warrant Officer 5	USN Chief Warrant Officer 5	N/A
Chief Warrant Officer 4	Chief Warrant Officer 4	USN Chief Warrant Officer 4	N/A
Chief Warrant Officer 3	Chief Warrant Officer 3	USN Chief Warrant Officer 3	N/A

Chief Warrant Officer 2	Chief Warrant Officer 2	USN Chief Warrant Officer 2	N/A
Chief Warrant Officer 1	Chief Warrant Officer 1	USN Chief Warrant Officer 1	N/A
Sergeant Major of the Army	Sergeant Major of USMC	Master Chief Petty Officer of the Navy	Chief Master Sergeant of the Air Force
Command Sergeant Major	Sergeant Major	Command Master Chief Petty Officer	Command Chief Master Sergeant
Sergeant Major	Master Gunnery Sergeant	Master Chief Petty Officer	First Sergeant Chief Master Sergeant
First Sergeant Master Sergeant	First Sergeant Master Sergeant	Senior Chief Petty Officer	First Sergeant Senior Master Sergeant
Sergeant First Class	Gunnery Sergeant	Chief Petty Officer	First Sergeant Master Sergeant
Staff Sergeant	Staff Sergeant	Petty Officer First Class	Technical Sergeant
Sergeant	Sergeant	Petty Officer Second Class	Staff Sergeant
Specialist Corporal	Corporal	Petty Officer Third Class	Senior Airman
Private First Class	Lance Corporal	Seaman	Airman First Class
Private	Private First Class	Seaman Apprentice	Airman
Private	Private	Seaman Recruit	Airman Basic
(*) Reserved for wartime only.			

SOURCES

Books

Andrade, John M., *Latin-American Military Aviation* (First Edition) (Earl Shilton, Leicester, UK: Midland Counties Publications Ltd, 1982)

Bosch, Brian: *Balaguer y los militares dominicanos* (Santo Domingo: Fundación Cultura Dominicana, 2010)

Butler, Phil & Dan Hagedorn, *Air Arsenal North America. Aircraft for the Allies 1938-1945. Purchases and Lend-Lease* (Hinkley: Midland Publishing Limited, 2004)

Cassá, Roberto, *Algunos componentes del legado de Trujillo* (Madrid: Iberoamericana Editorial Vervuert, 2001)

Chester, Eric Thomas, *Rag-Tags, Scum, Riff-Raff and Commies: The U.S. Intervention in the Dominican Republic, 1965-1966* (New York: Monthly Review Press, 2001)

Diederich, Bernard, *Trujillo, la muerte del Dictador* (3rd Edition) (Santo Domingo: Fundación Cultural Dominicana, 1990)

Dienst, John & Dan Hagedorn *North American F-51 Mustang in Latin American Air Forces Service* (Arlington, Texas: Aerofax, Inc., 1985)

Domínguez Tavera, Coronel Piloto Luis José, *Piloto Escuadrón de Caza* (1st Edition) (Vernon, British Columbia: Sunshine Graphics, 2015)

Doyle, David: *Standard Catalog of U.S. Military Vehicles* (Iola, Wisconsin, USA: Krause Publications, 2003)

Exército Brasileiro, *O Destacamento Brasileiro da Força Armada Interamericana na Republica Dominicana en 1965, FAIBRÁS* (Rio Grande do Sul, Brazil: O Tuiutí, May 2017)

Forslund, Mikael & Thierry Vallet, *Swedish Jet Fighter Colours* (White Series I. Rainbow No. 9135). (Sandomierz, Poland: Mushroom Model Publications, 2017)

Forty, George & Jack Livesey, *The World Encyclopaedia of Tanks & Armoured Fighting Vehicles* (Leicestershire, UK: Hermes House, 2012)

Gleijeses, Piero, *The Dominican Crisis* (Baltimore, Maryland: The John Hopkins University Press, 1978)

Hagedorn, Dan, *Latin American Air Wars and aircraft 1912-1969* (Crowborough, East Sussex, UK: Hikoki Publications, 2005)

Hagedorn, Dan, *P-38 in Latin America* (1st Edition. Kindle edition in English) (Aviation Art & History, 2022)

Hagedorn, Dan, *Republic P-47 Thunderbolt. The Final Chapter. Latin American Air Forces Service* (St. Paul, MN: Phalanx Publishing Co., Ltd. 1991)

Hagedorn, Dan, *Texan and Harvards in Latin America* (Staplefield, West Sussex: Air-Britain (Historians) Ltd., 2009)

Hagedorn, Daniel P., *Central American and Caribbean Air Forces* (Tonbridge, Kent: Air-Britain (Historians) Ltd, 1993)

Hellström, Leif & Dan Hagedorn, *Foreign Invaders. The Douglas Invader in foreign military and U.S. clandestine service* (Leicester: Midland Publishing Limited, 1994)

Higuchi, Hélio, *A Servicio do Generalíssimo. Os Pilotos Brasileiros na República Dominicana* (1ª Edição) (São Paulo: C&R Editorial, 2014)

Kurzman, Dan, *Santo Domingo: Revolution of the Damned* (New York: G.P. Putnam's Sons, 1965)

Legg, David, *Consolidated PBY Catalina. The Peacetime Record* (Shrewsbury, England: Airlife Publishing, 2002)

Lowenthal, Abraham F., *The Dominican Intervention* (Cambridge, Massachusetts: Harvard University Press, 1972)

Nuñez Fernández, José Antonio, *La Guerra de Locutores, Abril 1965* (Santo Domingo: Biblioteca Nacional Pedro Henriquez Ureña, 2009)

Ortega Vergés, Carlos M., *Aviación Militar Dominiacana, Evolución Histórica, 1910-2008* (Kindle edition) (Santo Domingo: Editoria de Revistas S.A., 2021)

Overall, Mario & Dan Hagedorn, *Douglas DC-3/C-47 in Latin American Military Service* (Manchester: Crécy Publishing Limited, 2021)

Palmer, Bruce, *Intervention in the Caribbean: The Dominican Crisis of 1965* (Lexington: University Press of Kentucky, 2015)

Puesan, Luis P., *La Historia de la Aviación Militar Dominicana. Desde sus inicios a su decadencia* (1st Edition) (Orlando, Fl: Independently published-Author's edition, 2022)
Rivas, Santiago, *British Combat Aircraft in Latin America* (Manchester: Hikoki Publications Limited, 2019)
Rocha, Jober, *A participação do Brasil na Guerra Civil da República Dominicana. Una epopéia da FAIBRAS* (Kindle edition) (Rio de Janeiro: Author's edition, 2014)
Sensión Villalona, Augusto, *La Dictadura de Trujillo, 1930-1961* (Archivo General de la Nación. Volumen CLXXXIII) (Santo Domingo: Editora Búho S.R.L., 2012)
Szulc, Tad, *Dominican Diary* (New York: Delacorte Press, 1965)
Vargas Llosa, Mario, *La fiesta del Chivo* (1st Edition) (Madrid: Editorial Alfaguara, 2000)
Walsh, Frank, *Dominican Crisis, 1965-1966* (Alexandria, Virginia: T.B.N. Enterprises, 1966)

Articles

Crasswelle, Robert: *"Trujillo: The Life and Times of a Caribbean Dictator"*, and John Bartlow Martin: "*Overtaken by Events: The Dominican Crisis from the Fall of Trujillo to the Civil War*". Articles published in the magazine *Political Science Quartely*, The Academy of Political Science. Volume 83. (Oxford: Oxford University Press, 1968)
Hagedron, Dan: *Latin Mitchells, North American B-25 in South America Part four*. Article published in the *Air Enthusiast Magazine*, England, issue #108, December 2003
Nanda, Ved P.: *The United States' Action in the 1965 Dominican Crisis: Impact on World Order.* Article published in the Denver Law Review, Volume 43, Issue 4, Article 2. 1966
Oliveira, Dennilson. *O Que Foi o Destacamento Brasileiro da Força Interamericana de Paz – FAIBRÁS* (Hoje-Paraná, Brazil - February 2023) *https://hojepr.com/coluna-dennison-destacamento-brasileiro-forca-interamericana-de-paz/*
Sánchez Barría, Felipe (2012). "*Reseña de la seducción del dictador: Política e imaginación popular en la era de Trujillo*". Article published in *Revista de Historia Iberoamericana* 5: ISSN 1989-2616

Documents

Fuerzas Armadas Dominicanas, *Manual de Doctrina Conjunta de las Fuerzas Armadas* (1ra. Edición) (Santo Domingo: Editores Impresores, S.A. N/D).
Gleijeses, Piero, *Hope Denied: The US Defeat of the 1965 Revolt in the Dominican Republic.* Working Paper #72. Cold World International History Project. Woodrow Wilson International Center for Scholars (Washington, DC, 2014)
Greenberg, Major Lawrence M., *The Army in Support of Political Initiatives: The 1965 Dominican Republic Intervention* (U.S. Army Center of Military History: Washington DC, March, 1987)
Greenberg, Major Lawrence M., *United States Army unilateral and coalition operations in the 1965 Dominican Intervention* (Historical Analysis Series) (U.S. Army Center of Military History: Washington DC, 1987)
Inter-American Peace Force/IAPF: *Stability Operations Report* (Public Affairs Office, Santo Domingo, Dominican Republic, 1966) (San Juan, Puerto Rico: Ramallo Bros. Printing, Inc., 1966)
Nalty, Bernard C., *The Air Force Role in five crises, 1958-1965: Lebanon, Taiwan, Congo, Cuba and Dominican Republic* (USAF Historical Division, Liaison Office, June 1968)
Ringler, Major (USMC) Jack K & Henry I. Shaw, Jr., *U.S. Marine Corps Operations in the Dominican Republic, April-June 1965* (Historical Division, Headquarters, U.S. Marine Corps: Washington DC, 1970)
U.S. Army 82nd Airborne Division: *Power Pack. Dominican Republic 1965-1966* (Command and General Staff College; Leavenworth, Kansas, 1971)
Wilson, Lamar C., *Estados Unidos y la Guerra Civil Dominicana. El reto a las relaciones interamericanas* (U.S. Naval Academy, Annapolis, 1967)
Yates, Lawrence A., *Power Pack: U.S. Intervention in the Dominican Republic, 1965-1966* (Leavenworth Papers #15) (Fort Leavenworth, Kansas: Combat Studies Institute, U.S. Army Command and General Staff College, 1988)

Interviews

Mrs. Magdalena Cubas, daughter of Colonel Roberto Cubas Barboza, Commander of the Paraguayan Contingent of the IAPF in the Dominican Republic in 1965-1966, in March 2024 in Asunción, Paraguay.
Mr. Luis Puesan, Dominican Aviation Historian, in May 2024 by telephone.

Web Pages

Dominican Air Force history at:
https://airforcedominicana.blogspot.com/p/historia-fuerza-aerea-dominicana.html?m=0/
U.S. Army Center of Military History, Armed Forces Expeditionary Campaigns: Dominican Republic, 28 April 1965-21 September 1966 at:
https://history.army.mil/html/reference/army_flag/dominican.html

ENDNOTES

Chapter 1

1 Ramfis and Rhadamés were names taken from characters in the opera *Aida* by Giuseppe Verdi.
2 Bernard Diederich, *Trujillo, la muerte del Dictador* (3rd Edition) (Santo Domingo: Fundación Cultural Dominicana, 1990).

Chapter 2

1 https://es.wikipedia.org/wiki/Ejército_de_República_Dominicana
2 https://es.wikipedia.org/wiki/Ejército_de_República_Dominicana
3 https://tanks-encyclopedia.com/
4 Hélio Higuchi, *A Servicio do Generalíssimo. Os Pilotos Brasileiros na República Dominicana.* 1ª Edição (São Paulo: C&R Editorial, 2014).
5 See *Cuban Military Aviation Volume 1: Organisation and Development of the Cuban Army Air Corps, 1913–1952,* also in the Latin America@War series, by the same author.
6 Luis P. Puesan, *La Historia de la Aviación Militar Dominicana. Desde sus inicios a su decadencia* (1st Edition) (Orlando, Fl: Independently Published-Author's edition, 2022).
7 https://fard.mil.do/sobre-nosotros/galeria-de-ex-comandantes/
8 https://airforcedominicana.blogspot.com/p/historia-fuerza-aerea-dominicana.html?m=0/
9 https://armada.mil.do/principal/historia-naval/
10 https://armada.mil.do/principal/excomandantes/
11 https://www.policianacional.gob.do/sobre-nosotros/historia/

Chapter 3

1 Bruce Palmer, *Intervention in the Caribbean: The Dominican Crisis of 1965* (University Press of Kentucky, 2015).
2 They did not call themselves 'Loyalists', it was a term given by the Americans during the civil war since they were 'loyal' to them.
3 The *Movimiento Revolucionario 14 de Junio* was founded in 1959 as an extreme left movement with an ideology based on anti-*Trujillism,* anti-imperialism, communism, Marxism-Leninism-Maoism, left-wing nationalism and populism. Initially they fought against the *Trujillista* dictatorship and then defended the Bosch government, fighting against the military junta in the civil war. This association was dissolved in 1968.

Chapter 4

1 https://history.army.mil/html/reference/army_flag/dominican.html
2 Ringler, Major (USMC) Jack K & Henry I. Shaw, Jr., *U.S. Marine Corps Operations in the Dominican Republic, April-June 1965* (Historical Division, Headquarters, U.S. Marine Corps, Washington DC, 1970).
3 DEFCON 1 (Defense Condition 1) is the maximum alert level, in the event of an imminent attack. DEFCON 2: armed forces prepared to be deployed and fight in less than six hours. DEFCON 3: increase in the preparation and mobilisation of troops. DEFCON 4: the activity of the intelligence services is slightly increased and National Security measures are tightened. DEFCON 5 refers to the normal situation in peacetime.

Appendix

1 https://mide.gob.do/insignias/
2 https://www.policianacional.gob.do/sobre-nosotros/historia/
3 https://www.defense.gov/Resources/Insignia/

ABOUT THE AUTHORS

Hélio Higuchi was born in São Paulo, Brazil on 12 November 1953. He graduated in Architecture and Urban Planning, with a postgraduate degree in Marketing, and has been working in the hotel sector. His main hobby is doing research on military history and its respective equipment in Latin American countries. He is the author of several books on Latin American military aviation and armoured vehicles, as well as numerous articles in specialised magazines from Brazil, the United States and England. This is his second book with Helion.

Antonio Luis Sapienza Fracchia was born in Asunción, Paraguay on 14 May 1960. He graduated from the *Catholic University of Asunción* where he got a B.A. in Clinical Psychology. He also took specialised English courses at *Tulane University* of New Orleans, Louisiana, and teaching methodology at *San Diego State University* in California. He is now retired but worked for nearly 40 years as an English Teacher and one of the Academic Coordinators at the *Centro Cultural Paraguayo-Americano* (CCPA), a binational institute in Asunción. Married with two children, he resides in the capital. He is an Aviation Historian and has written more than 500 articles in specialized magazines and web pages on the Paraguayan Aviation history and has given numerous lectures in schools, universities, institutes, military and civil institutions in Paraguay and abroad. Since 2004, he has been an aviation history professor in the Paraguayan Air Force (FAP). In May 2024, he was appointed Corresponding Academician of the Paraguayan Academy of History. He has published 30 books since 1996, this being his sixteenth with Helion. He received a total of seven decorations for his academic merits, two from Argentina, one from Brazil and four from his own country, Paraguay, two from the Air Force, one from the Naval Aviation and one from the Civil Aviation Authority DINAC.